NMLS SAFE ACT EXAM STUDY GUIDE - COMPLETE TEST PREP FOR MORTGAGE LOAN ORIGINATORS

WITH 200+ OFFICIAL STYLE QUESTIONS & ANSWERS TO ENSURE YOU PASS WITH EASE

KNG EDUCATION

CONTENTS

ALSO BY KNG EDUCATION

Audiobook edition available on Audible & iTunes.

Narrated by Will Stauff.

If you are new to Audible, you can use the following link to sign up and purchase the book at the same time:

https://www.audible.com/pd/B09Z3WG7KK/?source_code=AUDFPWS0223189MWT-BK-ACX0-306763&ref=acx_bty_BK_ACX0_306763_rh_us

ISBN'S & LICENSING

Ebook ISBN: 9781915363220

Paperback ISBN: 9781915363237

Cover Image Professionally Designed by 99Designs.

Vector image licensed by Shutterstock (1803684841)

For bulk orders, contact kngeducation.wm6d8@8alias.com.

INTRODUCTION

What is the NMLS?

The Nationwide Mortgage Licensing System (NMLS) is an online database used by agencies that regulate mortgage and finance to maintain licensing requirements.

An NMLS license proves that the Mortgage Loan Officer you are working with is qualified to provide you with loan advice in at least one state. They are also called loan originators. These licenses are renewed periodically.

Obtaining a mortgage is a complicated and arduous process since it involves heavy financing, so you must ensure the person guiding you knows what they are doing. One of the easiest ways of doing this, is to simply look up their NMLS number in the NMLS database.

For these officers to be qualified, they are expected to spend 20 hours completing educational courses before they are licensed, pass the national mortgage test, allow the NMLS to get their credit score, and provide fingerprints so that the FBI can conduct a background check. Even after licensing, they still have to spend 8 hours of continuing education every year and make sure their state licenses are always updated in the system.

Purpose of the NMLS

· It allows people to look up their loan officers and make sure they are authentic; that way, they avoid being cheated by fraudsters. You can check their licenses and the state they are authorized to operate.

· The system ensures that users find all the information they need in one place instead of having to look across states for the same thing.

· Officers need the database to send applications, upload their documentation and maintain their licenses in the system.

· The lenders who employ these officers use it to make sure they employ the right people and to make sure they keep their information updated as well.

The NMLS Exam

It is also called the National Test or the SAFE Mortgage Loan Originator Test. It is used to test people who want licenses to be Mortgage Loan Originators (MLO's).

To take the test, you need to follow these steps;

· Create an NMLS account so you can get a username and password. You will receive an email from the website telling you the next steps.

· Enroll for the test and pay the application fee. Usually around $110. There are other processing fees involved further in the process.

· Schedule an appointment for when and where you will take the test. The process differs depending on whether you take your exam at a test center or online.

· Complete the 20 hours of the comprehensive courses to prepare for the test. These hours are compulsory, and you must complete them.

How does the Exam work?

According to the CSBS (the Conference of State Bank Supervisors) report of July 2021, the pass rate for this exam currently sits at 53%. This is considered a high failure rate, meaning many people consider this test fairly difficult to pass.

The candidate taking the exam is expected to master a lot of information before taking the test. They must know everything a mortgage loan originator needs to know in order to effectively and compliantly serve their customers. Unless the candidate (you) are willing to dedicate the right amount of time to study, you may easily join the 47% that have to retake the exam. There is usually a 30-day waiting period before you can take the test again. If you fail it three consecutive times, then you have to wait six months before you can do it again.

The biggest problem with this test is that there is usually just not enough time to deliver all the necessary information. The knowledge required to effectively take this test should take around 150 hours, but is squeezed into 20 hours in 14 days. Where do people take the 20 hours, is it online or physical? As a result, the professionals taking you through the course are forced to skim through the coursework. This means that a lot is left for the candidates to figure out by themselves. This is why the candidates need to be dedicated to doing the extra work, otherwise it will all have been for nothing, and that is where this audiobook is designed to help you.

The majority of the people that have passed this test recommend that on top of the 20 hours you spend on the official coursework, you spend an extra 20 hours studying on your own. The more time you spend becoming familiar with the material, the higher your chances of passing once you get to the testing center. You will be required to have a high level of self-discipline to crack this, otherwise, you will think you have time to study and keep postponing until you wake up one day and there is no time left.

Unlike the tests we took in school, you will not have to wait for too long to know your score. Once you take this NMLS test, you will only need to wait 72 hours to get your test results. If you fail, you prepare to retake, but you can apply for your license in the NMLS database if you have passed.

Where to take the exam?

You can schedule your exam with the Prometric testing centers, which are scattered all over the country. Every state has these physical centers, so just choose the one closest to where you live. You can also choose to do it online through the Prometric ProProctor System. You will need to download the Proproctor app from the website for this.

Prior to the exam, you will need to provide identification documents and they have to be original. You will need a valid government-issued identification that has your photograph.

As with every exam, there are rules that must be adhered to, and the following apply when taking the NMLS exam;

- You cannot take the test for someone else.
- You cannot take any personal belongings into the exam room. If you are at a center, a locker is provided to leave your stuff inside of. If online, no one can enter the room while you take the test.

- You cannot give or receive any assistance, even on bathroom breaks.
- You cannot share the contents of the test with anyone.

Anyone found breaking any of the rules risks being denied a license or having their license revoked at any time.

Passing your Examination

To pass the MLO exam, you must score 75% and above - otherwise you will have to retake it.

Since the failure rate is fairly high, here are a few tips that will keep you from adding to it;

· Take Your Live Classes – These classes are made a requirement for a reason. You will have access to skilled professionals who have extensive knowledge of the field. Furthermore, you will also be able to ask questions while getting immediate feedback. This one-on-one interaction is the best way to make sure you get the best out of the sessions. Even though the time allocated for these lessons is not realistically enough, what you get in that limited time will help you out a great deal.

· Rest – A lot of us underestimate the power of a good-night's sleep. You may be inclined to pulling an all-nighter the day before your exam, but I highly advise against it. You will end up exhausting yourself, and you will barely have any energy for the next day which will increase your anxiety once you start the exam. Being clear-minded when you take the exam will serve you well. So make sure you study well throughout the study period so you can rest when it matters.

· Plan your exam time well – You may have heard someone brag about how they only used an hour to complete the exam, but that is not the competition you should be worried about. You might be able to finish in that same hour too, but make sure you don't rush through the test. You are allotted 3 hours to complete this exam so take your time to understand the questions and give the answers to the best of your knowledge.

· Look out for the 'negatives' – No test is ever straightforward, and there will be traps meant to throw you off, so be careful. You might encounter words like 'everything but', 'except for', and many others, so make sure you understand what the question is asking. Read it more than once if you need to. Missing one of these could cost you.

· Answer every question – When you leave a question blank, it is automatically wrong. So even if you do not know what to answer, just guess anything. You might just get lucky and select the right answer. Trust your gut - it might just know what you do not.

· Always choose the best answer – Sometimes, questions have more than one answer, and since you cannot choose them all, find the best one and choose it.

· Try to confirm your answers immediately – In this exam, you can either confirm, or confirm and review. When you confirm, it goes directly into the system as your final answer, but when you confirm and review, it is not counted until reviewed at the end. It's best to confirm all the questions you are absolutely sure about so you do not run out of time at the end, and all you have to go back through are the ones you did not confirm - as opposed to all of the questions.

· Simplify information provided – Sometimes, questions have too much information meant to confuse you, so instead of panicking, take a breath and break it down slowly until you get what you need to apply.

· Use Elimination – You will not know the answer to every question, but you may have an idea, so when you encounter a question like that, eliminate the answers starting with the least likely, and the one you remain with might just be the right one.

· Study on Your own – I cannot stress this enough. Use those 14 days to study your ass off. It is worth sacrificing those parties and movies just to squeeze in extra hours of study?

A bonus tip most people give is that you should avoid doing the exam immediately after you finish your coursework. There are some things that you can only comprehend after engaging in the field, so find someone to train you as if you are already working, or you could just observe them. Equally, you shouldn't wait too long either so that you don't forget what you already know.

Other requirements for a Mortgage Originator License

Passing the NMLS exam is definitely the main requirement, but it is not the only one. You will also need;

· A background check – The FBI will conduct a criminal background check on every candidate. You will be required to pay $36.25 for a live scan and $46.25 for the paper card capture. This check is conducted to make sure the applicant is fit for the job. Applicants get the results within 3-5 business days, but this is subject to change depending on the FBI processing time at that time. According to this check, you can be disqualified if;

- You are found to have been convicted of crimes such as fraud, money laundering, or any other that shows dishonesty.

- You have been convicted of any felony within the seven years you are filing your application.

- You have ever had your license revoked.

Anyone with these issues is advised to seek legal counsel before starting the process.

· Provide fingerprints – Unless you have already submitted fingerprints to the NMLS in the last three years, you will be required to have them taken. Apart from them accurately confirming that you are who you say you are, they are used by the FBI in your background check. The fee is included in what you pay for the background check.

The fingerprints will reveal everything about you; your date of birth, address, employment, and every basic thing about your life. To schedule your appointment, you must create a field print account. One set of your fingerprints will be collected and later deleted for data protection once submitted to the NMLS.

· Permit a credit report – Every candidate has to go through this authorization process, and the fee is $15 - which can be paid by either you or your employer. This report is meant to determine if the MLO is financially responsible. This, however, does not mean that you cannot become an MLO if you have bad credit. There is no official minimum credit requirement for the job.

· Processing fees – You are required to pay the NMLS $30 as setup fees once you start the process, as well as $30 as an annual processing fee.

· Legal Age – You must be an adult of at least 18 years and above.

How much does the exam cost?

The exam currently costs $110. That excludes the processing fees (previously mentioned) charged by the NMLS. The exam has 125 questions. 115 of them will count to your score, while the other 10 are just sample questions which will not count. Remember that you need to score at least 75% to pass, so you must get at least 87 questions correct, of the 115 being counted.

Differences between the varying states of America

The NMLS is nationwide, meaning it is legal in the entire US territory. This also means that as long as an MLO can meet all the requirements of a state and pass the NMLS exam, they can get as many licenses to practice in as many states as they want.

Being licensed in more than one state comes with benefits such as;

- Access to a larger pool of clients
- You can move with your clients
- You add to your credibility.
- You can compete with interstate banks.

To acquire a license in any state, you must meet the educational requirements. However, several states have specific elective requirements, so make sure you check beforehand.

Examples of different state electives include;

- Nebraska – 2-hour state PE

- Texas – 3-hour state PE
- Arizona – 4-hour state PE
- Utah – 15-hour state PE
- Pennsylvania – 3-hour state PE
- Louisiana – No state Elective required.

These electives are in addition to the 20-hour national requirement of coursework. You also have to remember that you have to maintain your license in all these states which are renewed annually. These processing fees may also vary from state to state. Apart from these, all the other rules are pretty much the same; they all follow the NMLS guidelines.

Reasons for not getting a License?

Several factors may cause you to be denied an MLO license, such as;

· Education Requirements

As mentioned earlier, applicants are required to complete 20 hours of official coursework and 8 hours of continuing education every year. Also, remember that some states require additional hours, so you must keep up with the requirements or you risk having your license denied or revoked.

· The Exam

Like we said earlier, the only way to get through the door is to pass your NMLS exam by getting 75% and above. Other requirements do not matter until you have this one done. Otherwise, you will not get your license.

· Your Background Check

The financial world is sensitive, so if your employer even imagines that you cannot be trusted, then you will not be employed. That is why anyone convicted of crimes like fraud and money laundering is denied a license. If you are convicted of any other crime, you must wait seven years to apply for a license.

· Credit Assessment

While there is no agreed-upon minimum credit score required to get this job, different states handle this aspect differently;

- Some keep a copy of the report but do not use it

- Some are declining applications of applicants with low credit scores

- Other states are asking applicants with a score less than 580 to write a letter explaining how they plan to fix their credit.

What does a Mortgage Loan Originator do?

A Mortgage Loan Originator (MLO) is also known as a mortgage broker. They are responsible for walking clients through the process of acquiring a loan through rating and pricing their mortgage.

These officials usually work for big banks, credit unions, and other lending institutions, but this does not limit many others to be self-employed officials and work independently. A lot of people tend to think a mortgage originator and a mortgage banker are the same person, yet they are not. A mortgage originator will show a client their loan options, but only a mortgage banker can approve or deny the application.

The elaborate roles of an MLO include;

· Collecting clients' financial information such as debts, taxes, etc.

· Evaluating whether or not a client is creditworthy and eligible for a mortgage loan.

· Walking clients through the mortgage options

· Solving issues that may arise during the loan application process.

· Researching on any new policies on Mortgage loans.

· Ensuring all the data is in line with both the local and national rules.

· Monitoring the application process and providing a report.

· Informing clients if their application has been approved or rejected.

Mortgage Loan Originators are different - so what makes a good MLO?

· Their rates and fees. This will greatly influence the kind of clients they get.

· Their knowledge of the current market - so that they can best advise on any discounts and incentives to ensure their client's long-term success as a homeowner.

· How they handle their processes in terms of technology. They cannot always expect their clients to be there physically. These days there are a plethora of apps that will allow people to approve contracts and sign documents remotely, and an MLO should be proficient in using them.

· Most importantly, they should be somebody clients are comfortable talking to. Somebody that has great interpersonal skills and that can talk to anybody. Someone that can be asked any question, any time a client has a concern. The process can get complicated, so communication with your client is crucial.

Why is the NMLS Important?

For everything regarding mortgages to run smoothly, there must be rules in place, otherwise people will do whatever they please. This is why the NMLS exists, to maintain order and calmness in the mortgage finance world.

It is important because;

· It provides a comprehensive database for licensing and supervising.

· It ensures that Loan Originators are accountable.

· It protects customers from mortgage fraud.

· It provides an efficient flow of information between clients and loan service providers.

· It creates a fair process in the approval or denial of Loan Originators.

CHAPTER ONE

GENERAL MORTGAGE KNOWLEDGE

A mortgage is an agreement you make with a lender giving them the authority to take your property if you repeatedly fail to pay back the money you have borrowed, plus the interest.

People take mortgage loans either to buy a house when they don't have sufficient funds to buy it in cash; or to extract cash from the value of a house they own already. This means that even though you are the homeowner, your lender has an interest in your home until the day you clear your debt. Many make the misconception that they own their home, when in reality - until they pay the final monthly payment, the bank has the ownership.

Qualified and Non-qualified mortgage programs - What's the difference?

A Qualified Mortgage Program

This is the kind of loan that a borrower is more likely to be able to pay. The lender does in-depth work to analyze the borrower's ability by looking into their finances to ensure that the borrower can afford the loan they desire.

Characteristics

· Disallows risky features which are present in unqualified mortgages, such as;

- Paying off the interest only, without reducing the amount you borrowed.

- Negative Amortization - where the loan amount increases even though you make payments.

- Balloon Payments are also not allowed; these are when you make small payments throughout your loan term and then a huge amount at the end of the term.

- The loan term cannot be over thirty years.

· Uses a Debt to income ratio, which means that the amount of your income that goes towards your debt is limited.

· The up-front fees the lender is allowed to charge you are limited, but they will also depend on the size of your loan.

· Provides lenders with legal protection if they were thorough in making sure that you could pay back your loan.

The main purpose of qualified mortgages is to protect borrowers from excess fees and to make sure that they do not borrow more money than they can pay back.

Types of Qualified Mortgage

· General – This is the kind of loan that follows all the characteristics of a qualified mortgage - such as having no risky features, ensuring the borrower can pay, and that the debt to income ratio stands at a maximum of 43% (meaning the annual debt can not be more than 43% of the annual income).

· Temporary – This has all the features of the general mortgage except it can be purchased or guaranteed by Fannie Mae (short for Federal National Mortgage Association). It buys mortgages from lenders and plays a crucial role in making mortgages more affordable. Another thing about this temporary mortgage is that it is not required to follow the 43% debt to income ratio.

· Small Creditor – This kind of mortgage is offered by a lender whose assets are less than $2 Billion and originate less than 500 mortgages a year. It's also similar to the general mortgage, except that it is available to borrowers with any debt-income ratio.

· Balloon Payment – As much as these payments are not permitted in qualified mortgages, some underserved areas such as the rural parts have authorization. This is because of the HELP Act (Helping Expand Lending Practises) in rural communities.

Advantages

· Lower down payments

· Lower interest rates

· There are many lenders available

· It is less risky

Disadvantages

· Extensive documentation is needed

· Very strict credit requirements

· Foreigners are not eligible

· Investors cannot finance more than 10 properties.

How to increase your chances of qualifying for a Qualified Mortgage?

· Fix your credit by paying bills on time, clearing off balances on your credit card, and by following other well-documented credit repair strategies.

· Find someone to borrow with, so you can meet the debt to income ratio.

· Pay a higher down payment, resulting in a lesser loan amount and monthly payments.

· Getting a side hustle that shows a continuous flow of income for two years may add to your qualified income and help save more money for a down payment.

· If you have a two-to-four unit home, you can charge rent on the other units and use it to qualify. You can pay a down payment of as little as 3.5% in some programs.

Conventional mortgage

Conventional mortgages are designed for residential property. They are issued by private lenders like banks, credit unions, etc. They are not government-backed but do follow the rules set by Fannie Mae and Freddie Mac.

They fall into two categories;

· Conforming – they follow Fannie Mae and Freddie Mac guidelines.

· Non-conforming – they do not follow these guidelines.

. . .

Lending rules set by these government agencies include;

· The borrower must have a credit score of around 640 or above, depending on the loan and other factors such as the debt to income ratio.

· The debt to income ratio must be under 43%, but it could be lower for anyone with a lower credit score.

· No major credit issues like bankruptcy.

· The down payments must be 3% or more. If you pay 20%+, you do not have to buy mortgage insurance.

· The loan total is $510,400 or less. This, however, varies according to the location. Some areas are affluent while some are rural, so the prices of the properties will be very different.

Government-Backed Mortgages

FHA Mortgage

It is a home loan meant to help modest borrowers buy a home. The Federal Housing Administration insures it.

The requirements include;

· That the down payment is as low as 3.5%

· A credit score of as low as 500

· A debt to income ratio of 50 % or less.

· You must pay mortgage insurance premiums.

· There is a limit to the amount you can borrow, depending on location.

· When you get the FHA loan, the house must be your primary residence. If you want to resell, then you do not qualify for this loan.

VA Mortgage

These are loans available to veterans and members of the military. VA loans are backed by the Department of Veterans Affairs. Aside from active members of the military and veterans, spouses of deceased veterans are also eligible.

VA loans have the following characteristics;

· They do not require borrowers to pay any insurance premiums or down payments. Borrowers do however pay a funding fee that ranges between 1.4% - 3.6% of the amount borrowed.

· The origination fee is limited to only 1% of the loan, and lenders cannot charge additional closing costs.

· You can only buy a home to live in, not resell.

· There are minimum property requirements, so not all properties are eligible.

. . .

USDA Mortgage

These are for rural homebuyers and are backed by the US Department of Agriculture. The USDA offers three programs;

· Loan guarantees – It can guarantee a loan so that you can get lesser interest rates. You might however have to pay premiums for mortgage insurance, if your down payment is little to none.

· Direct Loans – These are for those applicants that earn a very low income. When subsidies are available, they may pay interest as low as 1%.

· Loans and Grants for Home Improvements – These help homeowners upgrade their homes.

The requirements for these mortgage loans include;

· You must be a US citizen or a permanent resident.

· Proof of a dependable income for at least two years.

· A good credit history

· The home must be your primary residence.

· A debt-to-income ratio at a maximum of 41%. However, if you have a credit score above 680, you can get a higher ratio.

. . .

Non-Traditional Mortgages - Should this be in the unqualified section up next?

These are unique loans that are strangely neither conventional nor unconventional. They are easier to qualify for but are very risky for both the lender and the borrower.

Their characteristics include;

· Flexible/negotiable repayment terms

· Low credit score requirements

· Higher interest rates than usual

· Borrowers can defer their interest or principal.

Types of Non-traditional Mortgages

· Balloon Loans – Allow you to pay only a small amount of the loan monthly, and then at the end of the loan period, you are required to pay the full amount.

· Interest Only Mortgages – You only pay interest for a period of time, but you do not reduce or pay off the principal amount borrowed. It will be amortized in the meantime. The lump sum of the principal is then due at the end of the mortgage term.

· Payment Option ARMs – This option allows borrowers to choose how they want to clear their loan.

They can choose interest only, minimum and over-based payments, and the term of payment i.e. 30 years, 15 years, 4 years, etc. The amount will be fully amortizing, no matter the period. It is beneficial for those going short-term, but quite risky for borrowers seeking a long-term loan because the amount owed may keep increasing over time.

Sub-Prime Lending

Sub-prime lending refers to lending money to people with low credit ratings. Due to the high risk involved, the interest rates are much higher, and the requirements are now more stringent since the 2008 financial crisis - which was caused partly by banks lending to almost anybody, regardless of their financial status!

This kind of lending allows individuals who have no chance in the standard (prime) lending market to have a future of homeownership.

Some common characteristics of sub-prime borrowers are that they;

· Have low income

· Their debt to income ratio is often 0.5 or more

· Their credit history and credit score is poor

· They have delayed payments on their credit cards

· May have been bankrupt or facing foreclosure in the past

. . .

Types of Sub-Prime Lending

· Interest Only – The borrower only pays interest initially, and then the rest of the loan amount is due at the end of the term. The interest rate may be variable or fixed throughout, depending on the agreed-upon mortgage.

· Fixed-Rate – The interest remains constant for the entire period of the payment. However, the period of payment becomes much longer than average. While other loans may take 30 years, these can go for up to 50 years!

· Adjustable-Rate – The interest stays fixed at the beginning, but after a while, it changes to a rate that will vary with how the market and economy changes.

· Dignity Lending – The borrower pays 10% of the loan and accepts a higher-than-usual interest rate. If they show they are punctual with payments and prove that they are creditworthy, the interest is reduced to the standard rate.

Non-qualified Mortgage Programs

These programs do not have to meet as many requirements as a qualified mortgage. It is the kind of program used by borrowers with fluctuating income, such as the self-employed. They also suit those with possible credit issues like late payments, bankruptcy, foreclosure, etc.

Characteristics;

· The document requirements are more flexible.

· The debt to income ratio limits are more lenient.

· Borrowers can choose interest-only payments where they will only pay interest for a period of time without reducing the principal amount owed - whereas for qualified mortgages, this is typically not allowed.

· Less stringent requirements overall, so less paperwork.

Non-qualified mortgage programs offer products such as;

- Bank Statement Loans - Only bank statements are needed for these loans, and they are mostly used by the self-employed, entrepreneurs, etc. The borrower can sometimes qualify with only two months' worth of bank statements.
- Recent Credit Event Loans – This is offered to people who are facing a recent issue with

their credit, such as bankruptcy or foreclosure.

- No Income Investment Loans – These only take into account the rental income from a particular investment property and disregard your personal income.
- Foreign National Loans (ITIN) – The individual will have to provide a valid visa or visa waiver. They will also have to provide three active trade lines with a two-year history.
- Commercial Rental Property Loans – Caters to real estate investors that want to expand to single-family homes, condos, 20-unit properties, etc. The loans make it easier for "buy-and-hold" investors.
- Jumbo Loans with 10% Down – These are ideal for high-income earners looking to invest in other assets and to first-time buyers that are still dealing with student loans.
- Asset-Based Loans – This allows you to use assets such as cash in savings accounts or equities, as leverage for the loan.
- Interest-Only Home Loans – These have long terms that allow you to pay only the interest for the first few years while the principal owed remains the same.

Advantages;

· You can use alternative documentation or other assets to prove loan worthiness.

· Foreigners are eligible

· Relaxed credit requirements

· Investors can finance as many properties as they want.

Disadvantages;

· High down payments

· Higher interest rate

· They are more challenging to find without a good & knowledgeable MLO

MORTGAGE LOAN PRODUCT OFFERINGS IN DETAIL:

1. Fixed-Rate Mortgages

The interest rate for this loan is the same throughout the repayment period. The interest rate on a fixed-rate mortgage remains constant throughout the term unless the borrower requests a change through a refinancing program. The vast majority of mortgage loans have a fixed interest rate. This product is a common choice for homeowners who want a budget-friendly monthly plan that is stable, where they don't need to worry about economic changes affecting their monthly payments.

Fixed-rate loans are fully amortizing, which means that after the loan is completed and paid off, the buyer is free and clear of any principal and interest payments. In the early stages of a fixed-rate mortgage, the majority of the monthly payments will be used to pay interest. After the first several years, more of it will go toward the principal balance. As a result, the amount owing on your home will decrease more rapidly in the coming years.

Advantages

· The monthly obligations do not increase aside from any hike in taxes, bills, and insurance.

· You do not suffer an increase in interest rate no matter what happens in the market.

· Every month, you reduce the principal amount owed while owning a higher % of the house relative to the bank or lender.

Disadvantages

· The closing costs might be higher

· You take longer to repay the loan

· The interest rate may be higher than the market. For example, you may fix the loan at 4%, but if the base rate falls - other people may be able to fix new mortgages at 3%.

Common Term

The "term" of a loan refers to the amount of time a borrower has to pay back the principal and interest on a mortgage loan. There are several possibilities, each with its own set of benefits and drawbacks, and the term duration is usually determined when applying for a loan. You'll come across the following terms in your job or business as a mortgage loan originator:

- 30-Year: This is the most typical fixed-rate mortgage term and is the most common for borrowers and lenders. The lowest monthly payments are accessed through 30-year loans. However, you should be aware that you will pay more interest throughout the life of the loan, simply due to the compounding of the interest.
- 15-year: A 15-year term, on the other hand, will result in a reduced total interest payment throughout the life of the loan. However, because the same principal amount will be paid off in half the time, the monthly payments will be much greater, possibly causing more financial stress for the borrower if they have a low income. The good news is that the loan will be paid off much sooner than expected. The most usual terms are 30 and 15 years, but some lenders do provide alternative options..
- 20-Year: This is a term option that is sometimes available out there in the

mortgage finance world. You'll still be able to pay off your loan faster than if you went with the 30-year choice, but it'll be less expensive overall than if you went with the 15-year option.

- 10-Year: If you can afford much larger monthly payments and want to pay off your loan quickly, the 10-year term is a great choice for you. Before you pursue this path, be confident you understand the greater monthly costs.

The most significant benefit of short "terms" is that you will pay substantially less interest throughout the length of the loan. Borrowers should consider these options if they can comfortably afford the increased monthly payments. Here are some instances to demonstrate the distinction:

On a $240,000 loan, a 30-year fixed mortgage at 3% interest will cost you around $124,266 in interest over the life of the loan.

A 15-year fixed term, on the other hand, will cost you around $76,213, which is a big discount. Consider how much of a difference a higher interest rate would make, too.

A professional lender will go over all of this information with their clients and recommend the best solution for their specific needs and circumstances. While your monthly payments will remain largely consistent over the life of the loan, there may be modest variations year to year, depending on how much money is needed in your escrow account to cover property taxes and insurance. This number is usually not significant, although it is dependent on a variety of conditions. Home repairs, utilities, and HOA expenses are not covered by escrow accounts. A number of third parties, such as an agent, an escrow firm, and a mortgage provider, are in charge of escrow accounts.

You can save money on your monthly mortgage payments if you don't use an escrow account for taxes and insurance. You will, however, be responsible for making these additional payments on your own. It's easy to just bundle them with your mortgage, so you don't have to worry about any additional expenses or paying a huge sum at once.

2. Adjustable Rate Mortgages (ARM)

Although adjustable-rate mortgages are not as common as fixed-rate mortgages, they are nonetheless favored by some individuals. For these types of mortgages, there are possible savings opportunities. The rates are lower than fixed loans because you are not locking in a rate for a long time. They can be, at least in the beginning, a whole percentage point cheaper than a comparable fixed-rate loan. That one percent can add up to a lot of money saved, should interest rates stay low for the duration of the loan term.

An adjustable-rate mortgage does exactly what it says on the tin. The rate will fluctuate over time, and your monthly payments will fluctuate as well. The rate varies in accordance with current market conditions. Depending on the present situation, the rate may rise or fall. Some adjustable-rate mortgages are hybrids, meaning they are fixed for the first few years before modifying. After that, the rate usually varies from year to year. To familiarize yourself with hybrid loans, consider the following terms:

A 5–1 loan comes with a fixed rate for the first five years and then adjusts annually, afterwards.

A 7–1 loan has a fixed rate for the first seven years and then adjusts annually.

A 7–2 loan has a fixed interest rate for the first seven years and then adjusts every two years.

Adjustable-rate mortgages have, unfortunately, developed a terrible image over the last few decades. This mostly happened during the mid-2000s housing bubble. This was due to the fact that they included a number of features that allowed borrowers to get into serious financial problems. Artificially low beginning rates, for example, were simply teases by to tempt customers in. In the long run, however, they concealed the full cost of the borrowing. Prior to these concerns, these types of mortgages were fairly prevalent, and in many countries throughout the world, they are shockingly still the primary source of financing.

These risky features have mostly vanished in the USA today, and adjustable-rate loans are regaining popularity. They are, for the most part, straightforward and simple to comprehend, especially for borrowers looking for simple residential homes.

Many borrowers are worried that interest rates may spiral out of control. They are concerned, for example, about paying three percent one year and fifteen percent the next. This is an understandable concern. Fortunately, rate hikes are typically limited, and each modification can only increase the rate by a set amount. In addition, many mortgages have lifetime rate restrictions that limit how high the rate can go. As a result, during a term limit, the rate will never rise above the cap, which is reassuring to borrowers and gives some predictability. Make sure you're aware of your mortgage's yearly and lifetime limits.

It's also worth noting that rates can fall. Many consumers who bought houses before 2008 were able to take advantage of considerable rate reductions subsequently. Interest rates throughout the 2010s remained at rock bottom and are only now beginning to be hiked by the Federal Reserve, as we go into 2022 and beyond.

Advantages

· Low payments for the first five to seven years while the interest rate is fixed. For this reason, these products make sense for those who are sure they will have completed their payments before this fixed time comes to an end.

· It is more flexible, which makes it a good idea for anyone looking to move or planning to sell their house in the five years before the unpredictable times and variable rate start.

· There is sometimes a limit on how much the rate can change, thus protecting the size of your payment.

· If one day the interest rates falls, there is a high chance that your monthly payment will drop too, so you could use this extra monthly cash to pay down debt or for other lifestyle costs.

Disadvantages

· Once the adjustable period begins and the interest fluctuates, you may find yourself paying way more, and some borrowers may get trapped and be forced to foreclose.

· Some lenders charge a penalty if you choose to refinance or resell the home in the first five years, so look for a product that does not have such penalties.

· ARMs can be complicated, and if the borrower doesn't take time to understand them, it could prove risky if they can't keep up with their repayment plan.

3. Balloon Mortgages

Balloon Mortgages are a type of real estate loan where the borrower, at the beginning, makes smaller or in some cases, even no monthly payments, and then makes a lump sum payment when the loan period lapses. The borrower can either pay interest-only, or pay both interest and principle so that the lump sum, in the end, is smaller. They can also choose to pay off debt at any point during the term, should they find the cash to do so.

Advantages

· Lower monthly payments

· Allows you to own a home even though you do not need to put up much money at the beginning.

· It is a good way to keep your monthly costs down while you plan to fund the lump sum at the end of the loan period.

Disadvantages

· Very risky because unless you have a great refinancing plan or have a lot of money saved up, you might not be able to pay the lump sum - and the house would be foreclosed/repossessed.

· If the general economy causes the value of your property to go down, you will not be able to refinance, especially if you have not seen any equity gains during the interest-only period. You could find yourself in 'negative equity', which is where the amount you owe is greater than the value of the house.

Chattel Mortgage Balloon Mortgages

Chattel mortgages are used to purchase or refinance non-permanently attached residences. In comparison to a typical mortgage, these loans are usually substantially shorter. Processing fees and loan amounts are also reduced by up to 50%. The hefty interest rates that come with them, however, are a huge disadvantage. On these loans, the annual percentage rate (APR) can be up to 1.5 percent higher than on a regular mortgage. Chattel mortgages can be used to finance the following categories of assets:

Manufactured housing: A manufactured home built after June 15, 1976. They are permanently mounted on a metal chassis and must exceed HUD's minimum safety standards. Moving these types of homes after they've been installed can have an impact on the financing.

Mobile homes built before June 15, 1976, may not have been subject to certain safety regulations that were enacted subsequently. A mobile home is difficult to finance.

. . .

Modular dwellings must adhere to the same municipal construction rules as residences constructed on a specific piece of land. Among chattel property, modular homes are usually considered the best investment.

Interest-Only Mortgages:

Lowering a loan's monthly payments is a good approach to make a property more affordable. Lowering interest rates is one of the approaches, which will result in significant cost savings. An interest-only loan in which the borrower pays a low interest rate for the first few years, usually five to ten. During this time, the primary balance remains unchanged. Of course, if a borrower wants to move ahead, he or she can make payments toward the principal. After the first payment period has ended, the loan is re-amortized or recalculated to pay off the principal and interest before the end of the loan term. The modest monthly payments for the first few years are the principal benefit of an interest-only loan. This can make a lot of financial sense for people in certain situations, for example, those who want to buy a home but are still working to increase their income.

. . .

Borrowers who intend to live in their home for less time than the interest-only period may benefit from this sort of loan. Many homeowners also appreciate it since they may utilize these years to put money toward other investments, such as house repairs and upgrades, car purchases and other necessities, or college tuition savings. Finally, because mortgage loan interest is tax-deductible, you may be able to deduct the entire amount of monthly payments during the initial term if you're simply paying interest. Imagine being able to purchase a property and then equip it, upgrade the appliances, make required repairs, and design it whatever you want without breaking the bank. This is achievable since interest-only loans save you money on monthly payments.

Before embarking on this journey, you should be informed of the following disadvantages:

- They're riskier than regular loans, and they're only available in particular situations.
- You must still pay the whole principal amount if you paid interest during the initial period and then start making fresh payments when re-amortization happens.
- If it's an adjustable-rate loan, the interest rate could rise and your income could fall before the interest-only term ends.

Repaying an Interest-Only Mortgage

You must ensure that you can return your interest-only mortgage in full at the conclusion of the term if you have one. Here are some options to make sure you can:

- Perhaps you can put money into an investment plan that will allow you to pay off the principal at the end of the term; your financial advisor will be able to tell you if this is viable in your situation.
- Inquire with a financial advisor about investing in a plan that can be used to repay the capital at the conclusion of the term.
- Make some one-time or recurring overpayments on a monthly basis. Making small monthly overpayments on a mortgage might make a big difference at the end of the term.
- You can apply for a better mortgage rate, switch to a repayment mortgage, and repay your loan over a longer period of time, reducing your monthly payments.
- Set up a regular savings account into which you deposit a set amount of money each month and withdraw only when you are

ready to pay off the loan at the end of the term.

- Interest-only loans are no longer available from many lenders, and they were a major source of problems during the 2008 financial crisis.
- As a mortgage loan originator, you will educate your clients on the many mortgage and mortgage product options available.

4. Reverse Mortgages

A reverse mortgage is a terrific way for older homeowners, usually those aged 62 and up, to take advantage of the equity in their house. If a borrower owns their house outright or has a significant amount of equity to draw from, they can take out a portion of their equity and not have to pay it back until they leave. This may appear to be an odd tactic, especially after working so hard to pay off a loan, but there are certain benefits to consider. First, let me go through this choice in greater detail.

Homeowners who take up this form of loan will not have to make monthly payments and will not be required to sell their home, allowing them to remain in it. When the borrower sells the house or passes away, the mortgage must be paid in full. The Home Equity

Conversion Mortgage, or HECM, is one of the most well-known types of reverse mortgages. Even if a property is paid off in full, a borrower may not be able to borrow the total worth of it. The amount a homeowner can borrow varies depending on the age of the youngest borrower or the eligible non-borrowing spouse. It also relies on current interest rates, the HECM loan ceiling, and the current market value of the home. The older a person becomes, the greater their primary limit will be.

The interest rates on a variable-rate HECM can change. However, the borrower has the following options:

- If at least one of the borrowers keeps the property as their primary residence, the monthly payments will be equal.
- Equal monthly payments for a set period of months.
- A credit line that allows you to borrow money until it expires.
- A credit line with fixed monthly payments for as long as you choose.
- The house has an occupant. This can be done for a defined duration as well.

You will get a single lump-sum payment if you choose a fixed-rate HECM option. A reverse mortgage's interest continues to rise each month, and you'll need enough money to cover taxes, insurance, and home maintenance.

Advantages

· No monthly payments required

· Funds help the borrower cater to living expenses.

· The borrower's spouse can stay in the home even after the borrower dies.

· You can use this to repay an existing mortgage to avoid foreclosure.

Disadvantages

· You must pay insurance and property taxes.

· Subject to higher closing costs

What is the goal of a Reverse Mortgage?

A reverse mortgage can be utilized for a variety of purposes, some of which are shown below:

- Supplementing retirement income, which is advantageous as many pensions aren't enough.
- Covering the cost of home repairs, particularly if you no longer have a source of income. Even if you don't have to pay a

mortgage in your golden years, it doesn't mean you won't have to pay for major repairs.
- Unexpected medical costs, such as prescriptions.
- This form of mortgage can help a lot of elderly folks. This is frequently a better option than higher APR loans, such as a high-interest credit card.

Requirements for Eligibility

To qualify for a reverse mortgage, the principal homeowner must be 62 years old or older. If they have a spouse under the age of 62, they must meet the following requirements:

- Having a single principal lien to borrow against or owning a home outright.
- Any existing mortgage that isn't paid off with the reverse mortgage funds must be paid off with the reverse mortgage funds.
- The home must be used as the borrower's principal residence; it cannot be used for rental or business purposes.
- Property taxes, insurance, and other recurring payments do not go away. As a result, the

borrower must continue to make these installments.

- A borrower is required to attend a HUD-approved consumer information session led by a counselor.
- The property must be kept in good working order.
- One of the following homes must be used: a single-family residence, a multi-unit building with four or more units, a manufactured home constructed after June 1976, or a condominium or townhouse.

If seniors intend to take this road, they must budget properly to prevent running out of money too soon. The fees involved are something to be aware of. Interest rates will be greater than they would be on a regular mortgage.

Here's a rundown of the various types of reverse mortgages:

Home Equity Conversion Mortgage (HECM): These mortgages are insured by the federal government and have higher upfront charges. Only FHA-approved lenders can offer HECM's. The funds can be used for any purpose.

• • •

Proprietary Reverse Mortgage: This type of reverse mortgage is a private loan, not backed by the government. With these sorts of mortgages, you can usually get a bigger loan advance.

Reverse Mortgage with a Single Purpose: This is a less popular option than the previous two. Various charitable groups, as well as state and municipal government entities, provide them. These loans have a lower maximum loan amount since borrowers can only utilize them for a specific reason, such as making their property more handicap accessible.

The amount of money a reverse mortgage loan can provide depends on the market value of the home, the age of the borrower, current interest rates, as well as the type of reverse mortgage used. Other mortgages and liens on the property may be a barrier.

5. Home Equity Mortgages

These are also called second mortgages. It is when you borrow a specific amount of money using the equity you have in your home. The lender uses your home as collateral. If you do not repay within the time set, the lender can foreclose the house.

The amount you get and the interest will depend on your home's market value, credit history, and income.

Most lenders will not give you anything above 80% of the home equity.

Advantages

· They are much easier to qualify for.

· Low and fixed interest loans.

· The loan term is longer than most consumer loans.

· You can use the funds however you please.

· Predictable fixed monthly payments.

Disadvantages

· You now have an extra mortgage to pay for.

· You could lose your house if you do not pay.

· You will be required to pay closing costs that other consumer loans do not charge.

6. Interest-Only Loans

This kind of loan is a non-conforming loan which means it has no government backing and it is harder to find. It allows the borrower to only pay interest for the first 5-10 years while the principal amount remains unchanged. It can either be fixed-rate or adjustable-rate.

Advantages

· Low monthly payments at the beginning

· Lower interest if it is an adjustable-rate mortgage.

· You get to keep more money in cash.

Disadvantages

· The only way to build equity is to make additional payments to the principal.

· If the house value declines, the homeowner could lose the equity created after paying the down payment.

· When the interest-only period ends, the monthly payments may double or more.

7. Construction Loan

This is a short-term loan with higher interest that helps the borrower build a residential property. They usually last a year - upon which the property should be complete and a certificate of occupancy issued.

This is very risky for the lender because unlike with other loans where they can seize the home if you default, they do not have that option in this case - since the house may not be finished. As a precaution, they will have an appraiser check the construction at various stages, and if he/she approves, then the lender releases more money. These approval-based additional payments are called draws or tranches.

Advantages

· The terms are flexible

· You only pay the interest during construction

· The additional scrutiny from the lender enables you to make sure you follow the set schedule.

· You get to choose the kind of house you want, how you want to build it, and where.

Disadvantages

· Has more stringent requirements needed for approval

· Once the construction is complete, the monthly payments will be high because, unlike during construction when you were only paying interest, now you have to start paying the whole loan amount.

· Not many lenders will give you the whole loan at once, instead, you will get it in draws/tranches as the building is built.

· The interest rate is higher than a standard residential mortgage

TERMS USED IN THE MORTGAGE INDUSTRY [MINI GLOSSARY]

Mortgage Terms..

· Borrower – You become a borrower when you apply for a loan and are granted it.

· Borrower Default - Occurs when a borrower fails to pay back the loan as agreed.

· Collateral – This is the asset you pledge to the lender when you want to secure a loan. If you default on your payment, the lender will take the asset (or house) as collateral.

· Co-borrower – This is the person that agrees to pay back the loan with you. Typically a husband or wife.

· Co-signer – This person signs a loan to help someone with poor credit secure a loan. They risk damaging their credit if the person they are helping defaults. They will also be responsible for paying back the loan should the borrower default. Typically a parent or family member.

· Credit Score – This refers to your credit history and how creditworthy it shows you are. According to the FICO model, a good credit score should be at least 670.

· Fixed Interest Rate – This means that the interest charged on a loan will remain the same throughout the loan period.

· Grace Period – This is the period in which you are not responsible for making any repayments. The interest usually accrues through and you can choose whether or not to pay it.

· Hard Credit Check – This is a credit inquiry performed by lenders before they approve your loan. It may drop your score by at least four points and will remain on your record for two years.

· Installment loan – It is a loan that has a fixed repayment period which involves monthly payments until you clear it.

· Loan Amortization – It is the process of calculating how much you will pay as principal and interest in every installment.

· Loan Agreement – This is the legal contract between a borrower and a lender which contains all the details about the loan.

· Late Fee – This is the penalty you are charged when you are late in making a payment for your loan.

· Loan Deferment – This is like a break you ask your lender for when you face financial hardship and cannot keep up with the payments. The loan will however keep accruing interest, and the period of payment will extend.

· Loan Limit – This refers to the maximum amount of money a lender is willing to loan you.

· Loan Origination Fee – Some lenders charge this to cater to their processing and underwritings costs. This amount will be deducted from your loan amount.

· Loan Terms – This is the amount of time you have to pay your loan.

· Non-recourse loans – This is a loan that has been secured by collateral. However, the borrower is not personally liable.

· Prepayment Penalty – Some lenders will charge you this if you make early payments or clear your loan before the end of the term.

· Principal – This is the amount of money you borrowed as a loan. It does not include the additional interest.

· Recourse Loans – This is a type of loan attached to collateral, and in the event that the lender has to take it, they can take other personal belongings to offset the loan.

· Secured Loan – This loan is secured by collateral.

· Soft Credit Check – This is when you check your own credit or give a lender permission to do it. This would not affect your credit score.

· Unsecured Loan – This one has no collateral attached to it, so if you default, the lender cannot take any of your personal assets.

· Variable Interest Rate – It is the kind of interest that fluctuates depending on the benchmark rate you agreed with the lender.

Financial Terms..

· CFPB – Consumer Financial Protection Bureau. It was established to help consumers understand financial agreements.

· Gross Income – This is the total income you earn before any taxes or deductions are subtracted from your paycheck.

· Annual Percentage Rate (APR) – This is the total cost incurred yearly after taking out a loan, as a percentage. It includes the interest rate and other financial charges.

· Automated Clearing House (ACH) – This is a popular transfer network for electronic funds. It allows for money to be transferred directly between lenders and bank accounts. It is only available to borrowers that are not on any active payroll.

· Downpayment – This is the difference between the loan amount and the purchase price of the real estate. The downpayment is paid by the borrower. A $100,000 property price with an $80,000 loan would result in a downpayment of $20,000.

· Equity – This is the difference between the debt secured by a property and its fair market value. For example, the equity on a $150,000 valued property with $90,000 in debt is $60,000. This is illiquid until extracted.

· Interest – This is the consideration paid for using money and is usually in the form of money. It is expressed as a percentage. It can also mean a person's share in a property.

· IRS 1098 Mortgage Interest Statement – It is a statement a lender gives the borrower to show the total interest he/she paid the entire year.

· Loan to value ratio – It is the ratio of the balance of the mortgage to the value of the secured property. A $70,000 mortgage on a $100,000 home would be a 70% LTV ratio. The higher the LTV, the higher the perceived risk.

· Net Income – This is your income after all the government deductions and taxes have been subtracted.

· Prepaid interest – This is the interest paid on the mortgage from the date the loan was first taken, to the end of the month.

· Principal – This is the balance remaining on your loan.

· Back-end Ratio – It compares the borrower's debt and monthly expenses to his/her gross monthly income.

· Debt Consolidation – This is done through a cash-out refinance and is normally unsecured debt. A borrower can pay off most of his debts with one large loan.

· Discount Point – This is the upfront cost borrowers pay to secure a lower interest rate. It is equal to 1% of the loan.

. . .

Disclosure Terms

· Closing costs – Also called settlement costs. These are the fees and expenses incurred in the lending process and are paid at the end.

· Final Settlement Statement – A financial statement giving an account of all the funds used or disbursed when a loan was closing.

· Auditor's Report – This is an accounting statement that is filed after a foreclosure sale occurs. It shows how much was generated and how much is owed to the lender.

· Negative amortization – This means that the loan will not mature. Any interest payments not made will be added to your principal balance.

· Account Termination Fee – This is a fee charged when you pay your loan in full and terminate your home equity in the first five years.

· Appraisal Contingency – A sales contract which says the property has to appraise at a value equal to or greater than the price you are offering.

· Preliminary Disclosures – These are disclosure forms sent to a loan applicant according to Federal Law.

· Primary Residence – Where someone lives.

General Terms

· Mortgagee – The lender who holds the mortgage

· Mortgagor – The borrower who pays for the mortgage

· Anniversary Date – The day when the 12th payment is due.

· Community Property – This is property belonging to a married couple.

· Deed of Trust – Used to get payment for a promissory note.

· Loan Denial Letter – It alerts an applicant that the lender is not willing to give them the loan they want.

· Loan Underwriting – This is the process of analyzing the risk associated with granting a loan to a borrower.

· Refinancing – Paying off a loan and getting a new one. Often used to extract equity by increasing the LTV ratio.

CHAPTER TWO

FEDERAL MORTGAGE AND RELATED LAWS

In the United States, the federal government enacted five federal mortgage lending laws. Each law was designed to protect mortgage loan consumers. They provide guidelines, procedures, rules, and regulations, ensuring that all consumers have a fair and equal opportunity for mortgage lending and loan applications.

The five laws are:

- Equal Credit Opportunity Act, 1974
- Real Estate Settlement Procedures Act, 1974
- Fair Housing Act, 1968
- Fair Credit Reporting Act, 1971
- Truth In Lending Act, 1968

THE REAL ESTATE SETTLEMENT PROCEDURE ACT [RESPA]

Origin

Congress created the Real Estate Settlement Procedures Act (RESPA) in 1974 to enable accurate settlement cost disclosures to homebuyers and sellers. RESPA was also enacted to prevent bribes, limit the usage of escrow accounts, and remove abusive activities in the real estate settlement process. The Consumer Financial Protection Bureau (CFPB) is now in charge of enforcing RESPA, which is a federal law.

Definition of Mortgage broker.

According to the 2008 RESPA Reform Rule, a mortgage broker is any person or entity that provides origination services and acts as a middle person between a lender and a borrower for a federally related mortgage loan. The description includes entities that close a loan in their own name and table funds the transaction, a loan correspondent pursuant to Title 24 of the Code of Federal Regulations Section 202.8 for a program with the Federal Housing Administration, and exclusive agents that are not the employees of the lender. Mortgage loan originators must be acquainted with the prohibitions, limitations, and exemptions set forth by RESPA.

The purpose of the law

- To provide disclosure throughout the real estate process to help educate buyers to make better decisions and more easily understand the process and material provided to them.
- To enact the prohibition of unlawful practices by real estate professionals such as bribes and referral fees.

Applicable Loan Types?

RESPA only covers federally mortgaged loans such as

- Reverse mortgages
- Home equity lines of credit
- Lender approved assumptions
- Loans secured by liens
- Home purchase loans.
- Loans for property improvement

RESPA limitations and prohibitions and exemptions

For the protection of the customer, RESPA has a number of prohibitions.

Section 6 of RESPA gives borrowers consumer safeguards when it comes to loan servicing. If a borrower submits his loan servicer a "qualified written request" regarding the loan's servicing, the servicer must respond with a written acknowledgment within 20 business days of receiving the request. The servicer shall make any relevant modifications to the borrower's account and offer a written clarification about any dispute within 60 business days of receiving the request. During this 60-day period, the servicer may not provide information to a consumer reporting agency about any past-due payment or qualified written request connected to that time.

Individuals or groups of individuals may be entitled to damages and costs under Section 6 of RESPA if servicers are found to have breached the section's requirements.

8th section

RESPA Section 8 makes it illegal to give or accept anything of value in exchange for referrals of settlement service business relating to a federally backed mortgage loan. It also makes it unlawful to give or accept any part of a fee for services that are not rendered. Kickbacks, fee-splitting, and unearned fees are all terms used to describe these types of payments.

Section 8 violations are punishable both criminally and civilly. A person who breaches Section 8 might face a punishment of up to $10,000 and a year in prison, according to HUD. A person who breaches

Section 8 in a private law dispute may be accountable to the person charged for the settlement service for three times the amount of the charge paid for the service.

9th section

Section 9 of RESPA forbids house sellers from requiring home buyers to acquire settlement services from a certain entity as a condition of sale, either directly or indirectly. Buyers may sue a seller who violates this provision for 3x the total amount paid for title insurance.

10th section

The amount of money a lender can demand the borrower to maintain in an escrow account for the payment of taxes, hazard insurance, and other expenses related to the property is limited under Section 10 of RESPA. RESPA does not compel lenders to impose an escrow account on borrowers; nevertheless, escrow accounts may be required as a condition of some government lending programs or lenders.

RESPA also forbids a lender from charging an escrow account excessive fees. A borrower may be required to deposit into the escrow account no more than 1/12 of the sum of all disbursements due during the year, plus an amount to cover any account shortages. In addition, the lender may request a buffer of not more than 1/6 of the total disbursements for the year. Once a year, the lender must conduct an escrow account examination and advise borrowers of any shortages. Any amount in excess of $50 must be repaid to the borrower.

Section 1024.5 covers the applicability of the law. RESPA and this part apply to mortgage loans linked to federal laws, except as provided in paragraphs (b) and (d) of this section. Most loans need to comply with the requirements if they are federally related to mortgages. These exemptions include;

- Business purpose
- Temporary loans
- Secondary market transaction
- Loans for vacant lots
- Assumptions without lender approval
- Loan conversions

A lender may own partial interest in the real estate, mortgage, or title company. RESPA requires that when one of the entities refers the applicant to another affiliated provider - the loan applicant receives an Affiliated Business Arrangement Disclosure. This disclosure must include the details of the relationship, and the estimate for the service should be provided at the time of referral and no later.

Settlement Services

These are services provided in connection to a prospective or actual real estate transaction. They include:

- Mortgage broker fees
- Attorney fees
- Originator services
- Credit report
- Inspections
- Document preparations
- Services related to processing
- Mortgage insurance
- Property taxes
- Use of a settlement officer
- Hazard insurance

A lender must provide the borrower with the list of settlement service providers at the time when the loan estimate is provided..

Required borrowers' information on application

The borrower must include the following basic information upon application for them to be considered for the loan:

- Name
- Social security
- Address
- Loan amount
- Income
- Property value

An Overview of the Foreclosure Process

Foreclosure happens when the homeowner is no longer capable of repaying the loan. The judicial and non-judicial processes are the two ways to proceed with a foreclosure.

1. In order for the foreclosure process to begin, the lender must file a complaint in court.

2. The non-judicial process is completed without the involvement of a court, and the method is usually defined in the mortgage's power of sale.

Both strategies are possible in some states. In most circumstances, the foreclosure will take at least a few months, and borrowers will have a certain length of time to redeem the property before lenders can file a deficiency judgment against the owner for lost funds, depending on the area. Whether you are a borrower or a lender, it is vital to research the legislation in your state.

Homeowners do have some safeguards in place to protect them in certain situations. Consider the following scenario:

- They have the option of filing for Chapter 7 bankruptcy, which allows them to surrender the property without incurring any further debt or responsibility.
- The present terms of a mortgage, including interest, loan, value, and payment program, can also be amended through Chapter 13 bankruptcy.
- A Deed in Lieu of Foreclosure occurs when the foreclosing party accepts the owner's deed of real estate rather than proceeding with the foreclosure. A deficit balance will almost always be claimed by the lender.
- Homeowners can also seek help from agencies such as the Department of Housing and Urban Development, or hire a lawyer who specializes in foreclosure law.

Borrowers should do all possible to avoid foreclosures because they can cause a slew of problems, including lowering their credit scores, making it more difficult to obtain loans in the future, while likely losing their home. After a foreclosure, a borrower must wait at least four years to qualify for an FHA loan.

As a Mortgage Loan Originator, your responsibility is to ensure your clients understand what they are signing up for when they apply for a mortgage. It's vital that you assist them in determining the best option for their situation and that you also thoroughly educate them on the hazards associated with various types of mortgages. If you believe a loan is not right for your client, notify them right away and explain why. Make certain that you always act ethically and within the bounds of the law. While there is much assistance available for persons facing foreclosure, borrowers should not blindly trust anyone who appears to know what they're talking about. It is critical to seek assistance from credible sources. When seeking foreclosure assistance, stay away from these following scenarios..

- Paid courses, boot camps, and seminars: These businesses thrive on stealing money from financially distressed and desperate homeowners who are willing to go to any length to get out of their predicament. Unfortunately, the information offered in these courses is frequently available in the public domain, or it is incorrect and useless.
- Signing the title over to a foreclosure recovery program: You will lose your home, and your bank will sue you for fraud if you do this. Borrowers are not allowed to transfer their

real estate interests without the bank's permission.

- A business that buys real estate and then resells it: Borrowers are unable to simply repurchase the property they owe money on. To do so, they will need to take out a new loan that is far larger than the previous one.
- Someone professing to have bank contacts will come across as extremely affable and educated. But believe me when I say that it is a ruse. Furthermore, regardless of how "nice" a borrower is with the banks, a borrower will need to hire a lawyer or rely on legitimate sources for help to stop the foreclosure process.
- Companies requesting payment of the mortgage through them: The only method to assure that payments reach the bank is to make them through the bank or the bankruptcy trustee.

Unfortunately, there are many piranhas out there that prey on people at their most vulnerable. Many people, on the other hand, are willing to lend a hand.

Initial Escrow Statement

The initial escrow account statement must include the amount of the borrower's mortgage monthly payment and the portion of that payment that goes into the escrow account, as well as the estimated taxes, insurance premiums, and other charges that the servicer reasonably expects to be paid from the escrow account during the escrow account figuring year, as well as the anticipated disbursement dates for those charges. The amount that the servicer chooses as a cushion must be shown on the first escrow account statement. A trial running balance for the account must also make up part of the statement.

EQUAL CREDIT OPPORTUNITY ACT (ECOA)

1. ECOA permissible act

The Federal Trade Commission (FTC) enforces the ECOA, which aims to prevent credit discrimination due to race, nationality, marital status, religion, age, gender, or receipt of public assistance. These factors may not be used for the determination of creditworthiness. There is information that is justifiable to be questioned under the act. These include:

- Credit history
- Immigration status
- Permanent residence
- May ask if a client is receiving child support or alimony

1. Factors that can not be used to discriminate

ECOA prohibits discrimination in all aspects of the mortgage process on the basis of all of the following;

- Nationality
- Age
- Marital status
- Ethnicity
- Religion
- Gender
- Race
- Receipt of public assistance

The terms which may be used to describe individuals in which marriage is involved are limited to unmarried, married, or separated.

Disparate treatment is the treatment of an individual worse than others based on a protected characteristic such as gender, race, religion, etc. This would, for example, be a male being given a lower interest rate than females of the same application status.

1. Circumstances where a loan can be denied

Acceptable reasons include the applicants' inability to display creditworthiness but may also be related to the proposed property. Ordinary circumstances for denial may include:

- Poor credit score
- Insufficient assets
- Poor credit history
- Immigration status
- Lack of employment history
- Proposed property having unfavorable characteristics

1. Regulation B

Regulation B was instituted to protect applicants from discrimination throughout the credit process.

A creditor shall not make oral or written statements in advertising or otherwise, to applicants or prospective applicants that would discourage a reasonable person from making or pursuing an application.

It provides requirements to lenders for compliance. They shall not discriminate based on age, marital status, income from public assistance, ethnicity, etc.

Notifying borrowers of action taken

The creditor must notify the candidate whether the loan has been approved or declined within 30 days of receiving the completed application. They must provide specific reasons for granting or denying credit on terms other than those initially requested. Furthermore, they must also include detailed reasons why the creditor terminates the account, refuses to increase the credit limit or refuses to make modifications.

Adverse Action

This benefits both consumers and companies by increasing openness in the credit underwriting process and preventing potential credit discrimination by requiring creditors to explain why adverse action was taken. A creditor must provide a notice if it has taken adverse action:

- on an uncomplicated credit application
- on a completed creditor application
- on an existing credit account
- made a counter-offer to an application for credit, and the applicator does not accept the counteroffer.

Cosigner Requirements

The requirements for the cosigner must follow all the restrictions of discrimination regarding race, marital status, sex, etc. However, the creditor can dictate certain stipulations such as;

- Clear credit history
- Must live in the United States for the majority of the year
- Must be a relative to the borrower (parent, grandparent, children, siblings, inlaws, spouses, etc.)
- Must have a lower credit score and as little as 3.5% down
- If your cosigner is a close friend, you need to write a letter to your mortgage lender explaining the relationship and why your friend wants to help you.
- The cosigner must be able to compensate for the borrowers less than perfect credit.

Acceptable income for loan review

Lenders want to know that you'll be able to pay your mortgage, therefore they'll usually only accept you if your annual payments are less than 30% of your annual income. Speak to a lender if you believe your debts are manageable and you can afford payments of up to 30% of your income. A mortgage broker considers reliable sources of income such as a part-time pension, alimony, public assistance, social security, and others. However, the applicant is not required to submit alimony, child support, or separate maintenance as income.

Factors considered when determining creditworthiness

There is no particular instruction in Regulation B on credit analysis methodologies. Creditors can employ judgment-based procedures or statistically developed techniques like credit scoring. Section 1002.6(b)(5) gives recommendations on what income should be considered when determining an applicant's credit-worthiness. All sources of income, including part-time earnings, pensions, alimony, etc., must be included by the creditor. However, creditors do have the ability to assess whether or not revenue should be included based on its chance of continuing.

Prohibition of the evaluation of creditworthiness include:

- a creditor must consider any of the forbidden grounds, including age when evaluating creditworthiness, which is prohibited (providing the applicant is old enough by law)
- denying an applicant without a telephone listing
- a creditor cannot take into account the possibility of children affecting income
- part-time income from an applicant or an applicant's spouse cannot be discounted or excluded by a creditor.

Disparate Treatment

When statements reveal that a creditor explicitly considered prohibited factors like race, color, age, or gender in determining a loan amount, which is overt proof; or when non-discriminatory factors cannot fully explain differences in treatment between different borrowers, this can be seen as comparative evidence of disparate treatment. Even without proof of prejudice or discrimination, a difference in treatment is enough to establish disparate treatment. For example, if a lender chooses to offer credit counseling or advice, they must offer the same services to all applicants without discrimination.

Suppose someone is offered a loan for $300,000 and they are 30 years old, but another person is only approved for $250,000, and they are 25. In that case, this can be considered disparate treatment based on comparative evidence if there is no other non-prohibited criterion that explains why. A lender telling a borrower that they can't provide them a bigger loan because they are female is an example of overt unequal treatment.

If there is a disparate impact concern, the next step is to see if the act or policy can be justified as a business need. This cannot be based on a hypothetical example, and real proof must be presented in order to satisfy this requirement. Even if it is determined to be a commercial need, it may still be in breach of rules if a less discriminating act may achieve the same result. To show a lender's application of a regulation or practice that has a disparate impact in violation of ECOA, there is no need to find evidence of discriminatory intent.

Creditworthiness should be determined by income, expenses, debt, and general credit history. Other indicators that can be used to establish loan eligibility under ECOA include asking inquiries about immigration status and residency, credit history, and part-time or other retirement income. If, and only if, a spouse is involved in the transaction, the lender may inquire as to whether the borrower is married, unmarried (which includes divorced, widowed, or single), or separated. Any income that is found stable after examination is considered acceptable for assessing creditworthiness.

This could include income from work, whether full-time or part-time, seasonal income, self-employment revenue, investment income, retirement income, and more. The most common reasons for refusing a loan are creditworthiness or a problem with the property. Poor credit history, a lack of assets, a property with unfavorable features, a lack of employment history, and immigrant status are all examples of this. The borrower must get property appraisal reports or other valuations done promptly, or at least three business days prior to closing, whichever comes first.

The borrower has the option of opting out of the time-frame and receiving the appraisal at the time of closing. If the borrower waives the period and the transaction does not close, the appraisal must be delivered within 30 days. Any action that refuses to grant a loan in the amount or terms (unless a counter-offer is made and accepted), as well as the termination of, or unfavorable change to an account that does not affect every account in the consumer's class (such as if the consumer moves out of the area or the lender closes accounts under a certain credit limit), or a refusal to raise the consumer's credit limit - are all examples of adverse action under the Equal Credit Opportunity Act. Lenders are forced by the Equal Credit Opportunity Act to deliver notices of action within 30 days of receiving an application.

The notice must include the action taken, the lender's name and address, as well as the name and address of the federal agency that regulates the lender's compliance. It also requires the reason for the action, and the name, address, and phone number of the individual from whom the applicant can obtain the reasons within 60 days of receiving the adverse action notice (the lender then has 30 days after the request to provide the reasons). If a lender takes an application over the phone, the lender must ask for the applicant's name and address so that they can be notified.

The lender is no longer liable for informing the applicant of the loan decision if the applicant refuses to provide this information. If more than one applicant is present, only the lead applicant receives notices of action. If the information needed to make a decision is lacking from an application, the lender can decline the loan, advise the applicant orally that further information is needed, or submit a Notice of Incompleteness within 30 days. A Notification of Incompleteness is a written notice that specifies what information is required, sets a deadline, and states that if the information is not delivered, the application will be refused. To ensure that lenders respect the law, the Equal Credit Opportunity Act requires applicants to provide demographic information such as gender, ethnicity, and sex. If an applicant leaves this information blank or refuses to offer it, the lender must guess the information based on appearance or last name and indicate that the applicant did not provide the information on the loan application. The Equal Credit Opportunity Act requires loan originators to keep a loan application for 25 months after receiving notification of acceptance or denial. Lenders that violate the Equal Credit Opportunity Act (ECOA) face civil penalties for both actual and punitive damages.

TRUTH IN LENDING ACT (TILA)

The Truth in Lending Act (TILA) is a federal regulation which was enacted in 1968 to safeguard consumers while dealing with lenders and creditors. It protects borrowers from credit invoicing and credit card activities that are erroneous or unjust. On certain types of loans, it compels lenders to provide loan cost information for comparison.

Loans covered under TILA

This act applies to most types of credit including:

1. closed-end credit such as car loans and home mortgages
2. open-end credit such as credit card or home equity line of credit

Definition

The annual percentage rate (APR) is the cost of borrowing money each year. It's calculated as a percentage. It additionally includes other charges such as insurance for the mortgage, most closing costs, discount points, and fees for loan origination, which are not included in the interest rate.

Finance charges are any fees that represent the cost of credit or borrowing. It refers to the interest and fees charged on certain types of credit. Other fees, such as bank transaction fees, are also included.

Notice of Right to Rescind

The rescission right refers to a consumer's ability to cancel some types of loans. You do not have the right to cancel a mortgage once the closing documents are signed if you are purchasing a home with a mortgage. You do have until midnight of the third business day after the transaction to cancel a mortgage contract if you are refinancing.

The three-day timeline does not start until all three of the following events have occurred if refinancing a mortgage and want to cancel a mortgage contract.

1. You sign a credit agreement, sometimes referred to as a promissory note.

2. A truth in lending disclosure form is sent to you.

3. You are sent two copies of a notification informing you of your right to cancel.

Home Ownership and Equity Protection Act (HOEPA)

As an expansion to TILA, the Home Ownership and Equity Protection Act, or HOEPA, was enacted in 1994. This law was passed to stop unscrupulous refinancing tactics and closed-end home equity loans with exorbitant interest rates. Any of these that pass the HOEPA's high-cost average tests are subject to additional disclosure restrictions and requirements.

Additional disclosures must be made when a high-cost mortgage is obtained, certain loan terms must be avoided, and the consumer must be offered additional protections. This includes advice on buying a home. The majority of applicants for a mortgage loan must be given a list of counseling groups by creditors. A creditor must also confirm that an applicant got counseling prior to securing a loan with negative amortization, which implies that even if regular payments are made, the amount due does not reduce and will continue to rise because payments are insufficient to cover interest.

The following are examples of the types of transactions that are restricted or regulated by the HOEPA:

- Purchase-Money mortgages - those in which the seller lends money to the buyer directly.
- Refinancing
- Closed-End home equity loans
- Credit plans with no expiration date

There are several transactions that are not covered by the HOEPA rule. Some counseling guidelines, however, may apply. Here are a few examples of these deals:

- Reverse mortgages
- Loans for construction
- Loans originated and financed by a Housing Finance Agency
- Loans made through the Rural Development department of the United States Department of Agriculture.

If a transaction is found to be non-exempt from HOEPA coverage, the coverage tests listed below must be used to establish whether it is a high-cost mortgage:

- What is the annual percentage rate?
- What was the total cost of the transaction in terms of points and fees?
- What are the possible prepayment penalties imposed by the loan or credit agreement?

High Priced Mortgage Loans

High-priced mortgages have an annual percentage rate (APR) that is at least 1.5 percent higher than the benchmark rate, the Average Prime Offer Rate, for first-lien mortgages. It is 2.5 percent higher for jumbo loans, and 3.5 percent higher for subordinate-lien mortgages. If a mortgage loan meets or exceeds these limits, the lender is required to have the house evaluated by a licensed appraiser. At least three working days before the closing, the appraiser must send the report to the borrower. If a property is being "flipped," a second appraiser must be hired at no expense to the borrower to complete an evaluation. A "flipped" property is one that sells within 90 days with at least a 10% price rise or within 91-180 days with at least a 20% price increase. Refinancing a higher-priced mortgage cannot result in a greater amount, balloon payments, or negative amortization. For first-lien, closed-end, higher-priced mortgages on a principal residence, lenders are required to keep escrow accounts for property tax and hazard insurance for at least five years unless the mortgage is paid off sooner. The account may be canceled after five years if the loan-to-value

(LTV) is 80 percent or less and the borrower has made timely payments. Communities with master insurance coverage, such as condominiums, do not require escrow accounts.

Small creditors in rural or underserved areas may be excluded from having to keep escrow accounts.

Compensation for MLO

It's possible that loan originators aren't paid based on the parameters of a transaction. They may be paid for the amount of credit given to a borrower. However, this must be a set proportion of the credit value, and there may be a minimum or maximum compensation amount. Loan originators may also be compensated through contributions to a defined contribution plan, which is either a designated tax-advantaged plan or a component of a defined benefit plan.

Loan originators can also be compensated through a non-deferred profits-based compensation plan if the compensation is not directly or indirectly tied to the terms of a transaction, and at least one of the following conditions is met: (1) the compensation does not exceed 10% of the individual total compensation for loan originator, for the time period for which the non-deferred profit-based compensation under the plan is paid; or (2) the individual loan originator was a loan originator for ten or fewer transactions in the 12-month period preceding the compensation determination.

• • •

If a loan originator is compensated for a consumer credit transaction secured by a home, the remuneration can only come from the consumer. Any monies offered by another individual to assist the consumer in paying for the transaction must be included in this compensation.

TILA -RESPA Integrated Disclosure Act (TRID)

On October 3, 2015, the TILA-RESPA Integrated Disclosure Rule was designed to resolve various loopholes in TILA and RESPA. The previous sections on these statutes reflect many of the modifications made by this law. However, we'll go through them briefly here. Closed-end loans, inviting loans, loans secured by unoccupied land or 25 acres or more, and construction-only loans are all subject to the TILA-RESPA Integrated Disclosure Rule. Within three days after receiving a loan application, the following disclosures must be sent. The Mortgage Servicing Disclosure Statement, the CHARM booklet required for ARM transactions, the Consumer Financial Protection Bureau's "Your Home Loan Toolkit" (a step-by-step guide to what a borrower can expect throughout the loan process), and a list of 10 HUD-approved counseling agencies are all included. The Notice for Right to Rescind should be issued before the three-day rescission period begins, which is often at closing for owner-occupied refinancing. Closing Disclosures should be provided at least three working days prior to the scheduled closing. For escrow accounts that are designated as a condition of the loan, the Initial Escrow Statement must be submitted to the borrower at settlement or within 45 calendar days following settlement.

If there is more than one percent common ownership between the businesses, the Affiliated Business Arrangement Disclosure must be supplied when a recommendation is made to an affiliated business. APR and finance charges, projected closing expenses, the rate lock's expiration date, a note regarding whether calculated costs could change, loan details, applicant information, and the property address are all included in the Loan Estimate. On page two, section A of the Loan Estimate, origination fees are listed. Other loan factors, such as appraisal, assumption, insurance, late payments, loan approval, refinancing, and service, may be included in the Loan Estimate. Loan terms, expected monthly payments, and total closing and loan fees are all included in the Closing Disclosure. If there is a change in circumstances that affect closing costs, or if the borrower requests changes, or if the property value changes, or if the borrower is disqualified for the loan, or if there is a delay in indicating Intent to Proceed, or if there is a delay of more than 60 calendar days due to a construction loan - the Loan Estimate may be amended (if the Loan Estimate indicates that revisions can be made for this reason).

Extraordinary or unexpected circumstances, erroneous information or a change in information, or a customer request to adjust the loan rate or loan amount are all examples of changes in circumstance. The borrower's name, income, and social security number are required on a loan application, as well as the property address or ZIP code (if the address is unknown), the estimated property value, and the requested mortgage loan amount. If an application is missing information, the loan originator may contact you to obtain the missing information before sending the Loan Estimate. Borrowers are entitled to an appraisal report at least three days prior to the loan closing.

Origination costs, taxes, government fees, recording fees, transfer fees, prepayment fees for items like insurance or interest, first escrow payments required at closing, and other charges like real estate commissions or lender credits are all permissible fees and finance charges. Loan consummation is defined by TRID as the point at which a borrower becomes contractually bound by the terms of a loan. Acceleration is described as repaying a loan faster than the conditions of the mortgage agreement require.

The TILA-RESPA rule covers the vast majority of closed-end consumer credit transactions backed by real estate. For applications received after October 3rd, 2015, a creditor or mortgage broker must include this new integrated information. Regardless of whether an application was received prior to this date, certain limits apply, such as charging fees to a customer before they have received a loan estimate and stated their intent to proceed with the transaction.

- Providing written estimates of specific terms and costs to consumers before they obtain a loan estimate, without any written disclosure telling them that the terms and costs may change.

- Requiring the submission of papers to validate customer information on an application before delivering a loan estimate.

HELOCs, reverse mortgages, and loans backed by mobile homes and other non-attached properties are exempt from the TILA-RESPA standards. Loans made by someone who isn't regarded as a creditor are exempt from the requirement.

Overall, this new rule mandates that borrowers receive their loan estimate and closing disclosure paperwork in a timely and accurate manner. The disparities between the estimated and closing amounts are highlighted on these forms. On the Consumer Compliance Outlook Document, the Federal Reserve has issued a list of the most common TRID violations. The following are a few of the most obvious:

- General loan information: Items including the loan identification number, settlement agent, and file number were frequently left blank on the Loan Estimate and Closing Disclosure forms.

• Closing cost details: The Closing Costs Table revealed three significant types of violations. The first was failing to specify how many months the homeowner's insurance was to be paid for. The second was neglecting to name the individual who would be reimbursed for closing fees. Finally, the third is that there was no disclosure of which government entities received taxes and fees.

• Cash-to-Close calculations: The Loan Estimate and Closing Disclosure's "Calculating Cash-to-Close" table summarizes the amount of cash required to close. When comparing the amount altered from the most recent Loan Estimate, several lenders forgot to fill out the "Did This Change?" item on this table.

• Contact information: The final infringement was that certain elements of the required contact information section were absent from the closing disclosure.

If you notice any obvious violations such as these, or any other issues with the Loan Estimate and Closing Disclosure documents, contact the lender right away.

(FACTA) FAIR & ACCURATE CREDIT TRANSACTIONS ACT & (FCRA) FAIR CREDIT REPORTING ACT

In 1971, Congress approved the Fair Credit Reporting Act, which gave individuals privacy rights and accurate credit reporting. The Fair and Accurate Credit Transaction Act (2003) is a follow-up to the Fair Credit Reporting Act. The Federal Trade Commission is in charge of both (FTC).

The Fair Credit Reporting Act governs credit reporting agencies (CRAs), which are in charge of accumulating data from creditors, as well as how customers can dispute inaccurate information. Consumer dispute information must be verified by credit reporting companies (such as Experian, TransUnion, and Equifax). A credit report cannot contain false or unfavorable information for an extended period of time.

Bankruptcies, on the other hand, can stay on a person's credit history for up to ten years, while tax liens can only stay on a person's credit history for up to seven years after they've been paid.

Some portions of the Fair Credit Reporting Act also apply to creditors who report late payments to credit reporting agencies, such as credit card firms, auto lending businesses, or mortgage lenders. If a creditor reports missed payments to a credit reporting service, the consumer must be notified within 30 days, either in a separate notification or on the consumer's monthly statement. Consumers were compelled to contact credit reporting companies to dispute any mistakes on their credit prior to the Fair and Accurate Credit Transactions Act. Consumers can now contact a creditor directly and seek an examination of the information they reported under the Fair and Accurate Credit Transactions Act.

Until a resolution is found, the creditor is also prohibited from reporting any further negative information. Creditors, insurers, employers, and other entities that accept credit, insurance, employment, or rental property applications can all obtain credit reports. To request a copy of an applicant's credit report, employers would normally need written consent. However, formal authorization is not often required, such as when a condition in a loan application allows the lender to check an applicant's credit history. A consumer report is any type of communication of information that bears on an individual's creditworthiness, credit standing, credit capacity, character, reputation, qualities, or style of living, as defined by the Fair Credit Reporting Act.

This could include things like criminal records, schooling, employment history, rental history, driving records, credit histories, and even information from social media.

If a loan is declined due to information on a credit report, a notification of adverse action must include the information as well as the credit reporting agency's contact information. Within 60 days of getting the letter, the borrower is entitled to a free credit report.

Consumers can also get a free credit report from each of the three credit reporting agencies once a year, thanks to the Fair and Accurate Credit Transactions Act and the boom in identity theft. Creditors can develop their own credit evaluation method by taking a sample of random customers' credit scores, identifying similar risk factors, and assigning a weight to those factors to evaluate the risk factor associated with an applicant. They can also employ credit score businesses' generic credit evaluation methodologies. A fraud alert system has also been established under the Fair and Accurate Credit Transactions Act. If a consumer believes their identity has been stolen, they can call one of the three credit reporting agencies, and a fraud alert will be placed on their file. Before approving credit, creditors will take additional procedures to verify identity.

This fraud notice is valid for 90 days, and the consumer is entitled to one free credit report during that time. People who have had their identity stolen and have completed an FTC identity theft report at www.identitytheft.gov, or made a police report - can get a seven-year fraud alert. Those who have an extended fraud alert are entitled to two free credit reports per year from each agency. The Fair and Accurate Credit Transactions Act requires businesses to use equipment that only prints the last five digits of a credit or debit card number on receipts to prevent identity theft. Consumers can also request that only the last four digits of their social security number appear on their credit reports by contacting credit reporting bureaus. Businesses and people who preserve consumer reports must use suitable disposal techniques and exercise reasonable caution to avoid unauthorized access to the information.

It does not, however, require the company to dispose of the data — simply that it does so in a responsible manner if it does. Lenders are required by the Fair and Accurate Credit Transactions Act to present applicants with the National Loan Score Disclosure form, which informs them that their credit score is only one element in determining credit eligibility. According to the document, they can also contact the lender if they have queries about their application or the credit reporting agencies if they have questions about their credit score.

The Gramm-Leach-Bliley Act (GLBA)

Famously known as the Modernization Of Finance Act of the 106th Congress, the GBLA safeguards personal financial information. It is enforced by the Federal Trade Commission and applies to institutions or organizations that are not controlled by other federal or state laws, such as private lenders, check cashing services, or mortgage, title, and tax preparation services. The Financial Privacy Rule, Pretexting Rule, and Safeguards Rule are the three main sections of the Gramm-Leach-Bliley Act privacy requirements. Consumers and customers are subject to various criteria under the Financial Privacy Rule. Financial institutions and other organizations that receive personal financial information must adhere to these guidelines.

A consumer is an individual who obtains a product or service for personal use, whereas a customer has an ongoing relationship with the institution, according to the Financial Privacy Rule. Customers are better protected than consumers when it comes to their personal information. Customers, for example, receive annual privacy notices that allow them to opt-out of most information sharing, but they only receive this notice if the institution shares their information with a non-affiliated institution. These privacy notifications can be printed or sent via email. To safeguard consumers, the Pretexting regulation prohibits obtaining personal financial information under false pretenses. The Safeguards Rule mandates that all financial institutions regulated by the FTC install safeguards to protect their customers' personal information. Institutions that obtain consumer information directly from customers or through other institutions must comply with this requirement.

The institutions are also in charge of ensuring that their service providers follow the rules. Any personally identifiable financial information obtained from an individual in order to supply them with a financial product or service is considered non-public personal information. This could be data provided by a client in order to receive a product or service (such as their address or social security number), data received via a transaction (such as account numbers or loan balances), or data related to the use of a product or service (such as information from a consumer report). If the customer agrees and a confidentiality agreement is in place, non-public personal information may be provided to a non-affiliated third party. This is for the purpose of having one company provide services for another, such as a financial institution releasing information to a company that will mail statements.

The Federal Communications Commission (FCC) and the Federal Trade Commission (FTC) formed the Do-Not-Call Registry (FTC). It covers all telemarketers, with the exception of certain non-profit organizations that engage in interstate or intrastate communications. Individuals are allowed to register up to three personal phone numbers free of charge.

Telemarketers, on the other hand, can still contact registered individuals with written consent. If a telemarketer calls someone who has registered on the Do-Not-Call Registry and has not granted the company written authorization to contact them, the corporation could be fined up to $43,792 per call. Telemarketers can also be fined if they call between the hours of 8 a.m. and 9 p.m., leave a voicemail without a phone number, do not identify the company by name, leave a pre-recorded voicemail without an established relationship or written permission, or offer debt-relief services without providing a time frame for results, the amount of settlement money required, or information about missing payments with consequences (such as low credit score, lawsuit, or submitting the account to collections).

Even if a person's phone number has not been registered, they can request not to be contacted by a corporation again. Political campaigns, charitable calls, telephone surveys, calls from a business with which an individual has an established relationship (who may contact the individual for up to 18 months after the business has concluded), calls from a business that the individual has inquired about (who may contact the individual for up to three months), and calls from a business that has received written permission to contact the individual are all examples of exceptions to the Do-Not-Call Registry. Telemarketers must keep their own do-not-call lists up to date by scanning the Do-Not-Call Registry at least once every 31 days to delete phone numbers from customers who have registered their numbers. Telemarketers must also register and pay fees, or they risk being punished for making any phone calls, even if the numbers are not registered. If a telemarketer makes a mistake, they can submit proof to avoid fines if they can prove it. They must, however, have a written do-not-call policy, provide personnel training, keep accurate records, and visit the registry at least once every 31 days. Solicitation data must be kept for a period of two years. There are several rules that apply to fax numbers as well. Advertisers cannot send messages to fax numbers unless they have already established a business relationship with the recipient, or the fax number is publicly available, or they have the recipient's permission, and/or the message includes instructions on how to opt-out of receiving any further messages on the first page.

Acts and Practices Concerning Mortgages

Advertising (Regulation N) Advertisements must not misrepresent loan terms, fees and charges, payments and consumer savings, or extra or associated services. The terms of credit that are published must be easily accessible to the general public. Advertisements and accompanying papers are required to be kept for a period of two years. Regulation N trigger terms are identical to TILA trigger terms. Interest rate, down payment amount, loan payment amount, number of payments, payback duration, and finance charge amount are examples of these words. The APR and the amount, as well as the terms of repayment, must be revealed if any of these words are used.

Electronic Signatures in Global and National Commerce Act (E-Sign Act)

Allows customers to consent to the use of electronic records and signatures in lieu of a paper document. Institutions that utilize this technology must inform customers about their rights in utilizing it, how to withdraw consent, and what hardware or software is required to access the records. The consumer must be notified whenever the hardware or software requirements change. Borrowers who utilize electronic signatures and records must demonstrate their identification using email, phone numbers, social network IDs, access codes, knowledge-based questions, or encryption keys. Electronic records must be stored in such a way that correct reproductions can be made for future reference. A single copy of a unique, recognizable, and unalterable record must exist.

The USA Patriot Act

Following 9/11, the USA Patriot Act was enacted to aid in the monitoring of communications and money laundering activity that could have been used to fund terrorist activities. This law affects mortgage lenders and loan originators in various ways, the most notable of which is the requirement of picture identification from applicants. A borrower's name, address, birthday, and social security number or employment identification number must also be collected. Financial institutions will need to create a Customer Identification Program to verify all account holders' identities. Account holders' names must be checked against a government database of known terrorists and fugitives, and suspicious activity must be reported. Institutions must also record payments of $10,000 or more and have a policy in place to prevent money laundering. All records should be kept private, and all staff should be instructed to follow these regulations.

The Homeowners' Protection Act (HPA) (Also Known As The PMI Cancellation Act)

The Homeowners Protection Act was enacted in 1998 to give protection to people who purchase primary residences using Private Mortgage Insurance (PMI). PMI is usually required on conventional loans with less than a 20% down payment. The HPA, however, does not apply to FHA mortgage insurance premiums (MIP). If the borrower is not in default, the lender must discontinue PMI when the loan-to-value ratio reaches 78 percent (based on the initial value of the home). Provided the loan-to-value ratio exceeds 80%, the borrowers can request that PMI be canceled if they have a history of making on-time payments. Borrowers must be informed if PMI is required and how to cancel it at the time of closing. According to the

Homeowners Protection Act, they must also get annual notices outlining their rights.

The Dodd-Frank Act

After the 2008 financial collapse and recession, the Dodd-Frank Wall Street Reform and Consumer Act, named after Senator Dodd and Representative Frank, was passed in 2010. The following are some of the Dodd-Frank Act's objectives:

- To make the processes linked to federal regulatory agencies easier to understand.
- To give stronger protection to consumers
- To improve financial institution monitoring and management.

In addition, procedures for dissolving failed financial firms must be established. The Office of Thrift Supervision was abolished by the Dodd-Frank Act, and its activities were taken over by the Office of the Comptroller of the Currency. The bill also established the Consumer Financial Protection Bureau (CFPB), the Financial Stability Oversight Council, the Orderly Liquidation Authority, and the Federal Insurance Office (all of which monitor finance regulation statutes such as RESPA, TILA, and TRID). Restrictions for home financing transactions must be observed, according to the Dodd-Frank Act. When refinancing a higher-cost mortgage, it must not have a greater debt, balloon payments, or negative amortization. Further restrictions include:

- Not getting an appraisal from someone who was chosen, retained, or compensated by a mortgage broker or real estate agent;
- eensuring that the lender is the appraiser's client;
- Loan staff not discussing the valuation with appraisers (this does not apply to real estate agents);
- Loan staff or those connected to them not ordering an appraisal;
- Not specifying a desired or expected valuation (a sales purchase contract can be provided);

The Consumer Financial Protection Bureau (CFPB)

The Federal Reserve has provided funding to the Consumer Financial Protection Bureau. The head of the Consumer Financial Protection Bureau is appointed by Congress, which also has the authority to amend or dissolve the agency. The Consumer Financial Protection Bureau has a number of functions, including making lending paperwork easier to understand, preventing predatory lending practices, educating the public and financial institution personnel, and monitoring the risk levels of financial transactions. Consumer complaints, which can be reported at www.consumerfinance.gov, are also reviewed by the Consumer Financial Protection Bureau.

(HUD) Department of Housing and Urban Development

The major goals of the Department of Housing and Urban Development are to develop programs that provide affordable housing to the public, eliminate housing discrimination, and to establish environmentally friendly communities. Section 8 housing, rental assistance for the elderly, housing for the disabled, Community Development Block Grants, the Office of Fair Housing and Equal Opportunity, FHA loans, and the Government National Mortgage Association are just a few of the HUD initiatives (Ginnie Mae). Borrowers who take out a high-cost mortgage must meet with a HUD-approved counselor for counseling.

A Housing Counselling Disclosure should be issued to the borrower, which lists ten HUD-approved counseling agencies in the area. The Fair Housing Act, which creates seven protected classes of people who cannot be discriminated against in residential housing transactions, is enforced by HUD. Race, color, religion, sex, national origin, handicap, and familial status are the seven aformentioned categories.

BANK SECRECY ACT (BSA)

Financial institutions are required to file reports regarding particular financial transactions and other activity under the Bank Secrecy Act and the Anti-Money Laundering Law. The Financial Crimes Enforcement Network (Fin CEN), a section of the US Department of Treasury, examines these reports. Suspicious Activity Reports (SARs) must be filed by financial institutions subject to the Bank Secrecy Act when customers or employees report suspicious or illegal activity (including computer hacking). Suspicious Activity Reports must be reported within 30 days after discovering the behavior or activity, unless no suspect can be found, in which case the institution might wait another 30 days to try to find the suspect.

The financial institution, on the other hand, must file within 60 calendar days. Even if a subpoena is issued, the information included in a Suspicious Activity Report must stay confidential. Companies must also file a Currency Transaction Report if they make a cash purchase of $10,000 or more in a single day, or if they make a deposit, withdrawal, currency exchange, or other payment or transfer to a financial institution that involves a cash transaction of $10,000 or more. Individuals who move more than $10,000 in cash into or out of the United States must file a Report of International Transportation of Currency or Monetary Instruments, or face civil or criminal penalties. Individuals having brokerage accounts, mutual funds, or foreign bank accounts must file a Report of Foreign Bank and Financial Accounts with the IRS once a year.

To guarantee national banks are effectively managing and delivering requisite alerts to law enforcement to deter criminal behavior, the Office of Comptroller of Currency (OCC) will lay down regulations, perform supervisory operations, and also initiate enforcement actions, if necessary. Terrorist funding, money laundering, and other financial institution abuses are examples of these practices. The OCC conducts monthly assessments of various financial institutions to ensure that they adhere to the anti-money laundering provisions of the Bank Secrecy Act (BSA).

Criminals have historically utilized money laundering to conceal or purify the source of monies gained through deception. These schemes constitute a significant threat to the financial industry's safety and soundness in the United States. Terrorists are also exploiting money laundering tactics to support their operations, putting the country's security under threat.

Under the BSA and related anti-money laundering rules, banks are required to:

- Implement appropriate BSA compliance programs.

- Establish customer due diligence processes and monitoring methods.

• Check against the Office of Foreign Assets Control, which imposes economic trade sanctions in accordance with US foreign policy and national security objectives.

• Establish a procedure for monitoring and reporting questionable activity.

• Develop risk-based anti-money laundering programs: The US Department of Justice provides banks with extra tools and resources to help them strengthen their BSA/AML risk management procedures.

A closer examination of Suspicious Activity Reports (SAR)

SARs, or Suspicious Activity Reports, must be filed using the BSA E-Filing System. A financial institution is required to file a SAR no later than 30 calendar days after the initial discovery of facts for filing occurs. A financial institution can delay filing and sending a SAR for an additional 30 calendar days if no suspect was identified on the original detection date. This gives the financial institution more time to identify a suspect. There can be no more than 60 days of delay in total.

Financial institutions are required by the BSA to help government agencies detect and prevent money laundering through the following three ways:

• Keeping track of cash purchases of negotiable instruments, which are signed documents that promise a certain amount of money to a specific person or their assignee.

• Keep track of any cash transactions that total more than $10,000.

• Any action that could be considered criminal should be reported.

Patriot Protection Act

The Patriot Act was enacted in 2001, which altered the BSA. The most significant change as a result of this was the requirement for financial institutions to have a Consumer Identification Program, or CIP. The CIP's goal is to authenticate the identity of borrowers and applicants, as well as to alert law enforcement if suspect individuals or actions are discovered.

On a mortgage application, the following information is required:

• Identifying information

• Birthday

• The individual's or their next-of-residential kin's or business addresses; or an Army Post Office

If the application is a corporation rather than an individual, the principal address for the local office, place of business, or some other physical location must be provided. An individual tax identification number will be used as the customer identifying number for inhabitants of the United States.

Alternatively, one of the following must be given by non-US residents:

- ITIN (individual taxpayer identification number)
- The number of your passport and the country from which it was issued
- The number on your alien identification card
- Any government-issued photo ID document proving nationality or domicile, including the number and county of issuing

CHAPTER THREE

MORTGAGE LOAN ORIGINATORS ACTIVITIES

Mortgage loan originators have several responsibilities in the real estate market, including;

· Conducting interviews for all mortgage applicants

· Participating in business development

· Maintaining a network with real estate professionals

· Preparing documents for loan submission

· Evaluating credit reports

· Administering mortgage loans and other specialized loan products

· Assisting customers with any loan-related queries.

· Setting up debt payment plans

For a borrower to be approved for a mortgage loan, the following qualifications are necessary;

1. Proof of income – The buyer must provide income statements and tax returns from the last two years, recent payslips to show income and year-to-date income, and proof of any extra income like bonuses or alimony.

2. Proof of assets – The buyer will need to provide statements from the bank and their investment accounts to show that they have enough funds to pay the down payment, closing costs, and other cash related costs.

3. Employment verification – For employed borrowers, the lender will call their current employer to verify their job, or their previous employer if they recently changed jobs.

However, for the self-employed, the following will be evaluated;

- The nature of the business and where it is located

- The product's demand

- The financial stability of the business

- Tax returns from the last two years

4. Other Documentation – The borrower will have to provide a copy of their driver's license, their social security number and allow the lender to pull their credit report. Additional paperwork may be needed as the process continues according to the requirements of the lender.

5. Credit report – Anybody with a high credit score is likely to enjoy a lower interest rate, while those with a poor credit score will be required to pay a larger down payment and pay higher interest over the term of the loan. Lenders prefer a credit score of 620 and above, but some will still work with individuals below that.

When you are in the mortgage loan business, it can be pretty challenging to land clients since not a lot of people are looking to get mortgages at any one time. The best way to win is to network like your life depends on it - the best people to create relationships with are local real estate agents. They are always handling people looking for homes so they can connect you with potential clients very easily.

However, some loan officers have proven untrustworthy to real estate agents primarily because of their empty promises, so some things you should do to build a strong relationship with real estate agents are;

· Demonstrate your knowledge of the industry – The agents need to know that they are working with somebody who knows what they're doing. Show them that you can guide them through the whole process, whether the borrower is experienced or a first-time homeowner.

· Add value to your emails – Since agents get a lot of emails a day, make sure the emails you send add value and are not just another email the agent can ignore.

For example, you can send weekly interest rates as well as updated product offerings.

· Use Social Media – Real estate agents rely on social media to get clients so make sure you have established a strong presence on these platforms. That way you can provide them with exposure and other co-branded activities. This will sweeten the deal for both of you.

· Live up to your promises – R.E agents only want to work with lenders who they are sure will provide their clients with exactly what they need, so you will have to find a way to back up your promises.

· Have a local presence – You need to show the agents that you know all about the local market, and you can meet their clients face to face when necessary. Create a strong network in your local market.

· Be available – Give agents your contact and never miss their emails, calls, or messages. Some officers actually spend a day or two a week in the agent's offices being at their beck and call, making it easier for them to give them any clients that come by. However, never attend their open house unless they have invited you, it is considered disrespectful in the industry.

However, real estate agents are not the only way to attract clients. Loan officers use several marketing strategies to attract clients, and they include;

· Find your niche – While it is not a bad idea to be a jack of all trades, it's best to be a master of something.

That is the only way you can determine your expertise. As an officer, ask yourself what kind of customers you want to help the most. Once you figure this out, you will better leverage your expertise when marketing yourself. For example, this could be construction loans, Chattel mortgages, or any other product type identified earlier.

· Use referrals – This is the most effortless method because you already have a network of clients. These clients are the ones to give you the referrals you need, and you can encourage this by;

- Asking them to give you reviews and testimonials after you serve them

- Consider sending them videos every year on the day they bought the house so they can remember how they loved working with you and that you are still around, should they or their friends need to use your services again.

- Check-in now and then on holidays or birthdays.

· Video & Email campaigns – These are usually short videos providing useful information for free. For example, the best takeout spots in town, the most attractive sites in the area, etc. These show that you care and you know what is going on.

· Use Real Estate Agents – Once you create a strong relationship with these agents, you will never lack clients. They will be providing you with as many as you could imagine since they are in contact with people looking to buy homes with mortgages on a daily basis.

· Use virtual events – Not everyone has the time to meet these days, and some people don't like to, so make sure you can reach them no matter where they are. The best way to do this is to host online sessions via Zoom where you provide useful information about mortgage loans.

· Use Social media – Social media platforms will help you connect with so many people from all over the world. You can advertise yourself by posting on your pages or by commenting on other people's posts, videos and tweets.

· Create a blog – When you start a blog, it means that you are providing information for free. To keep your readers engaged, make sure the information you provide is detailed and engaging. That way, you will stay at the top of their minds for when they are ready to buy their home.

Qualification, Processing, and Underwriting

Borrower

The borrower is defined as the person who takes a loan from a lender so that they can buy a property or multiple properties. Once you accept this loan, it means you are prepared to pay back the lender all the money within the agreed amount of time, usually plus interest.

As a borrower, there are many factors which come into play once you take the loan and during the process of repaying it. These factors include.

· Assets

An asset is any resource that has economic value owned by either an individual or an organization. When it comes to mortgage lending, assets are used as collateral by borrowers when acquiring a loan. This means that in case the borrower cannot pay back the loan on time, then the lender will take control and own this asset. The lender uses the asset's value to determine how much money they will lend you. This is called the loan-to-value ratio.

Advantages to the borrower

- They can get loans easier and quicker
- Low-interest rate

Disadvantages

- Borrowers can lose their property if they fail to pay the loan

Advantages to the Lender

- The loan is less risky due to being asset-backed

When a borrower signs the loan agreement, they accept the liability to repay the debt, including the interest that comes with it.

In case you find yourself in a position where you are unable to repay this loan, you should;

- Contact your lender before the due date so you can make alternative arrangements and arrange some kind of payment plan.

- As for a grace period so you can get your finances in order, and show them your plan.

- In case your current situation is permanent, you can renegotiate the terms of your loan and have the loan term extended

If you fail to report to your lender when your finances get tough and you end up defaulting, you may suffer the following consequences;

- If you have secured the loan with an asset, then the lender will take possession of it.

- For the loans not secured by collateral, the lender can get a court order authorizing them to take your personal possessions in order to sell them.

- The lender can go after your co-signer and demand they pay the loan.

- The creditor can also get a court order to have the debt directly paid by your employer through your wages. This means your salary will no longer come to you.

· Income

When buying a home, make sure you know how much will be deducted from your monthly income towards the loan payment. As much as every borrower's situation is different, the two most common deductions are 28% and 36%. This means that the borrower's housing payment, which also includes the principal, interest, insurance, and taxes - should never be higher than either of these percentages of their gross income.

The 28% is known as the front-end ratio (mortgage-to-income ratio) of the total housing costs of the borrower compared to their income, while the 36% rule is the back-end ratio or the debt-to-income ratio.

FHA, Fannie Mae, and Freddie Mac also have their own maximum ratios used by lenders. For conventional loans, it can be between 43-45 percent. These percentages can sometimes go higher.

· Credit Report

There are three credit scoring models created by FICO that lenders use to determine a borrower's creditworthiness. The three models are;

- FICO score 2

- FICO score 4

- FICO score 5

The mortgage lender will get a report from each one & then use the middle score to make the lending decision. However, for loans not secured by Freddie Mac or Fannie Mae, exceptions can be made, and you may get a mortgage with no credit score or poorer credit history.

When reviewing your credit history, lenders will go as far back as six years. They will look at how good you are at paying your debts on time, if you have ever missed any payments or if you have any outstanding debts.

Credit scores vary between 300-850. If you have a score above 650, then you are fine, but if it's below 620, then you will find it hard to get loans at favorable interest.

· Qualifying Ratios

These are the financial ratios that mortgage lenders use to determine if a potential homeowner is qualified for a mortgage loan. There are two types, front-end and back-end ratios.

They may also be referred to as the 28/36 rule, where lenders prefer that you do not spend more than 28% on the front-end ratio or more than 36% on the back-end ratio.

The front-end ratio (or the housing expense ratio) affects the loan underwriting phase, while the back-end ratio (or the debt-to-income ratio) affects the underwriting of personal loans and housing mortgages.

· Ability to repay mortgage rules

These are the factors that lenders consider when determining if a borrower will be able to repay the loan or not. They include;

- The borrower's employment status.

- Their current income or assets (except the collateral), which they will depend on when paying back the loan.

- The amount of the mortgage loan.

- If there are any other loans tied to the property.

- Any current expenses on the mortgage loan or property such as insurance.

- If the borrower has other debt obligations like child support.

- The debt-to-income ratio, each month

- The borrower's credit history

. . .

Tangible net benefits

Tangible net benefits are the financial advantage gained by a client when he/she refinances their mortgage loan, i.e. they are taking a new loan.

Some of these benefits include;

- Reduced monthly payments

- Lower interest rates

- A reduced loan term

- Cash-out benefits i.e. converting your home equity to cash

Appraisal

An appraisal is a professional's unbiased assessment of the property's market value. An appraiser is a professional who provides objective, impartial, and unbiased views on real-estate values. Lenders use appraisals to determine whether a property is suitable for use as collateral for a loan. Fannie Mae requires lenders to guarantee that appraisal reports are completed appropriately and without the involvement of a third party with any vested interest. Instead of being compensated based on the property's appraised value, appraisers are paid flat fees for this purpose. The Federal Housing Administration mandates a restricted house inspection in conjunction with the appraisal report, and the VA has a list of approved appraisers that work on a rotating basis. A Small appraisal is defined as one that is conducted for a property with two to four units.

Appraisal of Residential Income Property

The Dodd-Frank Act prohibits lenders from influencing appraisers. The lender cannot have a direct or indirect financial appeal in the assessment company for any home loan (including ones that the lender does not sell).

The following are some of the responsibilities that appraisers perform:

- They conduct market research in order to identify trends and local features.
- They stroll through the house from room to room, noting the general state of the interior, as well as the building materials used, such as carpeting, hardwood flooring, granite worktops, and the HVAC system, roofing, windows, and appliances.
- They draw out a floor plan of the property and take measurements of the exterior to determine the total living space.
- In the appraisal report, they identify any infractions of health or safety codes.
- They conduct research on similar properties that have sold in the nearby area in order to

determine the home's value or fair market value, as well as to verify and reconcile market data.

These duties assist the appraiser in determining the home's market value, which is the best estimate of what the property may sell for in an arms-length transaction in a competitive, open market. Depending on how much time has passed after the appraisal, the lender may request a further recertification of value by doing an exterior examination and conducting desktop market research to confirm the property's value has not declined.

When determining the value of a property, appraisers pay close attention to the property's highest and best usage. A property's use must be legal, physically possible, and financially feasible. While these factors are taken into account while evaluating residential properties, they are also beneficial when analyzing non-residential assets. The appraiser may, for example, examine whether a structure should be replaced with a new one.

Methods of appraisal

The Market Approach, Income Approach, and Cost Approach are the three most common and basic appraisal methodologies.

- The Market Approach (also known as the sales comparison approach) is best for residential and vacation homes.
- The Income Approach is suited for investment properties
- The Cost Approach is for new construction and special-use properties.

All three strategies are based on the Substitution Principle, which argues that a consumer will not pay more for a comparable property.

The Market Approach entails comparing the subject property to at least three recently concluded transactions of properties with similar attributes. The comparable properties will, in most situations, not be identical to the property being evaluated. This is because property is not fungible, so no two can be the same. If the comparable property has a better feature than the subject property (such as a finished basement versus a non-finished basement on the subject property), the appraiser will need to make a negative dollar adjustment to the comparable property's sales price in order to make it as comparable as possible to the subject property. If the comparable property has a lower-quality feature than the subject (for example, a one-car garage vs. the subject's two-car garage), the appraiser will add a positive dollar adjustment to the comparable's sales price to compensate for the discrepancy. The appraiser's purpose is to make the appropriate modifications so that the comparables are as similar to the subject property as possible in terms of attributes. The ultimate reconciliation of the comparable value and weight will be determined by a number of factors, including how recent the comparable sales were, which comparable properties had the fewest net modifications, and whether or not the comparable was located in the immediate neighborhood.

The appraiser's ultimate opinion of worth/value is based on their previous experience, education, and market expertise. Finally, some appraisers may use active listings to evaluate if a market is in a depreciating or appreciating trend.

The Income Approach calculates a property's value based on the yearly net operating income or investment return that a buyer anticipates from the property. The IRV formula is used, where I is the annual net operating income and R is the return on investment, or cap rate. V is the property value. The other two variables can be rearranged by basic algebra to calculate each variable. I =R*V; V = I/R; and R = I/V (*100 to make it a percentage).

Here are the algebraic equations in a simpler format:

Income ($) = Return/Cap rate (%) * Value ($)

Value ($) = Income ($) Return / Cap Rate (%)

Return / Cap rate (%) = Income Value

For example, if I (annual net operating income) is $40,000 and R (capitalization rate) is 8%, then 40,000 divided by will equal V (the property value) = $500,000, which provides us an estimate of the property worth based on the two figures we know. This was done by dividing $40,000 by 0.08, which is equivalent to 8%. To enhance their return on investment, a buyer must either pay less for the property than it is worth (buy below market value) or raise the property's cash flow by adding units or raising rents.

The Cost Approach calculates a property's value based on the reproduction or replacement of structures on the property, taking into account depreciation, the cost of renovations and construction, and the land value. The property's worth is the sum of costs minus depreciation plus the value of the land. Physical degradation (because of aging or poor upkeep), functional obsolescence (due to an obsolete design), and economic obsolescence are all examples of depreciation (due to external factors of the property, such as a deteriorating neighborhood). An increase in value that occurs as a result of an improving neighborhood, upgrades, or a rising market is known as appreciation.

The appraiser must assess the property's value using at least two of these approaches, according to the appraisal report. Each method will almost certainly yield a different estimate. As a result, the appraiser will have to reconcile the values before arriving at a final value. The Uniform Residential Appraisal Report, which lets the appraiser submit a value for each appraisal technique, is required by Fannie Mae. The appraiser will explain why they believe that value is the most appropriate. The gross rent multiplier (GRM) can be used to quickly calculate the property's value. The neighborhood GRM is calculated by dividing the average sales price of comparable neighborhood homes by the average monthly rent in the region. It is then multiplied by the monthly rent of the subject property to arrive at the subject's market value. The GRM equals 200 if a comparable house sells for $240,000 and the monthly rent is $1,200. As a result, the estimated value of a $2,000 rent property is $400,000 if the GRM stays the same, since the property is in the same area. The gross income multiplier (GIM) is similar in that it employs the same calculations, but instead of using simply the rent, it uses the rent plus other money generated by the property (such as vending machines or washers and dryers).

Some appraisal reports may include information about minor repairs or construction that won't be finished until after the loan is funded. The lender may proceed with the closure in certain circumstances, but all parties must agree that the construction will be completed within 180 days of the closing. The appraiser should factor in the cost of the remaining construction as well as the property's final worth. The appraiser, on the other hand, should avoid making dollar-for-dollar modifications. Importantly, the cost of the remaining construction must not exceed 2% of the "as-completed" value.

A completion escrow must be established by the lender, which will hold at least 120 percent of the expected cost of remaining development from the purchase proceeds (unless the contractor offers a fixed price, which only requires the lender to hold the exact amount (100%) of the remaining improvements). An escrow arrangement between the lender and the borrower will establish how the monies are disbursed. Once a certificate of completion is secured, the creditor will release the final draw from the escrow account. Within three business days of applying for a loan, loan applicants should have the right to get a copy of the appraisals. When lenders get appraisal results, they should endeavor to provide them to the borrower as soon as possible. Appraisal reports must be received at least three days prior to the closing date. To be accepted for official usage, appraisals must be required by the lender for loan purposes. Homeowners can obtain appraisals for a variety of reasons, including general value, estate valuations, pre-listing appraisals, and divorce appraisals.

Factors that may affect the value of your home during appraisal include;

· Any health or safety hazards

· The structural integrity of the house.

· Any improvements or upgrades you may have done.

· Cracks or stains on the walls or floors.

Title Reports

This refers to a document showing a property's legal status regarding who owns it. They are one of the most important things you should check when buying a house.

When buying a house, the first thing you will do is o buy title insurance. There are two policies;

- Owner's title insurance – protecting the buyer

- Lender's title insurance – protecting the lender

The owner's policy will protect the buyer in case of a problem after the title search is finished.

A title claim investigator will look for any claims that may have been made on the title so that your purchase is not affected. Some of these claims may include;

- Forgery

- Undisclosed owners or heirs.

- If a contractor never got paid after construction of the house

Once all these issues are solved and you buy the house, you get your own title. If you ever misplace it, you can get another at the clerk's office in the county where the house is located. In case you have taken a mortgage on the property, then your lender must have a copy of this title.

Insurance

For properties in flood zones, the National Flood Insurance Program (NFIP) provides low-cost, federally-subsidized flood insurance. The Federal Emergency Management Agency (FEMA) is in charge of the NFIP. It also creates Flood Insurance Rate Maps, which show flood-prone locations. The National Flood Insurance Program provides a maximum of $250,000 in coverage for a residential property with one to four units, as well as $100,000 in coverage for the contents of the house.

The lower figure of either 100% of the structure's replacement cost, the maximum authorized coverage from the NFIP, or the outstanding mortgage debt, determines the coverage amount for a specific property. Flood insurance was generally either unavailable or too expensive prior to the National Flood Insurance Program. Flood insurance is necessary for properties that are located in flood-prone zones.

Borrowers, on the other hand, are not required to ensure their personal belongings. Lenders must examine whether or not a property is in a flood hazard area before making a loan. Based on danger levels, FEMA assigns ten flood-zone ratings. A Flood Certification Fee must be paid at closing to cover the costs of determining whether a lot or property is in a high-risk flood zone. The National Flood Insurance Program insurance is offered but not required for homes in Band X or C and X. Flood insurance is needed for properties in zones A, AE, A1 to A30, AH, AO, AR, A99, V, VE, or V1 to V30. Some regions are classified as flood zone D, indicating that flood dangers are unknown.

Some borrowers may opt for private flood insurance, meaning it is offered by a company that is not backed by the government. Private flood insurance providers may be able to offer larger coverage levels or lower costs to some lenders. Private corporations, on the other hand, may have lengthy claims processes or be unable to afford huge disasters. Similar to the mortgage insurance payment seen on FA loans, private mortgage insurance (PMI) protects the lender if a borrower defaults on their mortgage (for non-FHA loans). When taking out a traditional loan with a down payment of less than 20%, the borrower is usually obliged to pay PMI, as mentioned earlier in the book.

While some borrowers may believe that paying for PMI is primarily for the benefit of the lender, it can also benefit the borrower. It may make it easier for consumers to qualify for lower interest rates and loans while having lesser down payments, for example. The cost of private mortgage insurance rises in tandem with the loan's loan-to-value ratio, therefore the higher the loan-to-value ratio, the higher the private mortgage insurance premium. PMI can be paid in a number of ways, as follows.

The majority of the time, it is included in the borrower's monthly mortgage payment. However, some borrowers pay for PMI upfront at closing. The final option is to combine upfront and monthly premium payments. The borrower can request that the lender abolish the PMI after they have 20% equity in their house (or an 80 percent loan-to-value ratio). If they don't, the lender must terminate the PMI when the loan-to-value ratio drops below 78 percent.

Fire, windstorms, hurricanes, hail damage, vandalism, and other natural disasters are covered by hazard insurance. In order to protect their investment, the lender will require you to get hazard insurance when you take out a mortgage. Fannie Mae will not buy mortgages with a hazard insurance deductible of more than 5% of the policy's face value. On the day of closing, this policy must be in place.

The closing agent is in charge of checking that the policy fits the lender's standards, that the owner's name and address on the policy are correct, and that the lender is protected by the loss payable provision. The lender must be designated as a loss payee on the insurance policy in order for the borrower to access the insurance money for repairs. Technically, government mortgage insurance is not a sort of insurance. In the case of FHA, VA, or USDA loans, the government's support protects the lender against losses in the event of failure or foreclosure. Lenders can require borrowers to obtain certain types of insurance, but they can't require them to be purchased from a specific insurance firm. If the borrower refuses to obtain insurance or stops paying their insurance premiums, the lender may select a business and charge the cost to the borrower's monthly statement. This is referred to as "forced insurance."

Closing Agent

The purpose of title insurance is to protect the property owner and lender against any harm or property loss that may occur as a result of liens, encumbrances, or flaws in the title to the property. Undiscovered liens, faked documents, fraud, concealed heirs, and recording errors are all possible defects in title records. A fault is defined as anything that occurs after the loan is closed that calls into doubt the borrower's right to own the property.

Liens are paid, and legal fees are covered by title insurance. Before issuing the title insurance policy, the title insurance provider will investigate public records for obstructions, as previously stated. Involuntary liens, for example, would have to be paid before the title could be transferred to a new owner.

At closing, voluntary liens are either paid off or assumed. The title commitment is a document that informs the borrower of any known flaws in the property as well as their right to possess it. A property survey, which is a drawing of the property that indicates the perimeters and positions of structures on the site, may be required by the lender or title insurance company. An encumbrance is a form of defect that occurs when there is a claim or restriction on the use of the property.

Setbacks, encroachments, easements, and restrictive covenants are examples of encumbrances. An easement is a legal document that allows someone other than the property owner to use the land for a defined purpose.

Utility easements, for example, provide utility employees the right to be on the property when they are needed. After the borrower has paid off their loan, the deed and title are transferred to them. This is known as a reconveyance deed. There are numerous occasions where reconveyance is not correctly recorded, resulting in title report flaws.

At closing, title insurance premiums are paid as a one-time cost. A lender's policy (one that protects the lender) and an owner's policy (one that protects the owner) are the two sorts of policies. Back taxes, liens, and competing wills are the most common claims filed against a title. A homeowner's insurance covers the entire purchase price, whereas a lender's policy just covers the loan amount. Although the lender's title insurance policy is necessary, the owner's title insurance coverage is not. Generally, whoever pays for the policy chooses the title company. RESPA makes it illegal for a lender to require a borrower to acquire title insurance from a certain company. The policy of an owner is non-transferable, which means that if the title is transferred, the new owner will need to acquire their own insurance. The lender's policy is transferable, therefore if the lender sells the mortgage to a secondary market investor, the policy will be transferred too. The American Land Title Association (ALTA), which was created in 1907, regulates the abstract and title insurance sector. ALTA also helps title insurance firms standardize their forms.

Settlement or Closing Agent

To ensure that the Closing Disclosure is correct, the settlement or closing agent must collaborate with the lender. They are in charge of compiling the closing statements and submitting them to the lender for approval. At least three business days before closing, the borrower must be able to see the Closing Disclosure. Everyone with an ownership stake (even if their income isn't utilized for qualification) must sign the security document at the end. In some places, the security instrument must also be signed by the spouse or domestic partner. Although a power of attorney can be used for closing, it is usually only approved when there are no other options. The power of attorney for the lender must also be provided by the attorney-in-fact. The lender may also be required to record the usage of a power of attorney with the security instrument.

Real estate transfer taxes, the appraisal fee, prorated mortgage interest payments, lender fees, any origination costs, property survey, title search, title policy, and credit report charges are all common charges and fees that appear on the Closing Disclosure.

Title insurance fees may be included on the Closing Disclosure

In many circumstances, the seller will cover the cost of title insurance if the buyer requests it. The buyer, on the other hand, is responsible for the lender's title insurance policy. Fees that must be paid in advance, as well as cash held in escrow accounts for various purposes, are referred to as prepaid fees. Prepaid items such as homeowner's insurance premiums, real estate property taxes, and per diem interest may be included in the loan estimate. Loan origination fees, which can range from 0.5 to 1% of the loan amount, are used to pay underwriting and processing costs.

Documents Explanation

The promissory note, mortgage, deed of trust, or security instrument; deed for property transfer; Closing Disclosure; Initial Escrow Statement; and the transfer tax declaration are some of the documents utilized throughout the closing process. The promissory note is the legal document that binds the borrower to pay back the debt. The mortgage, deed of trust, or other security instrument which gives the lender a legal right to the property if the borrower does not repay the loan is what gives the lender a legal right to the property if the borrower does not repay the loan.

The property transfer deed is the document that transfers ownership of the property. The Closing Disclosure is a document that lists all of the fees and charges related to the loan. The Initial Escrow Statement explains how much the borrower will have to pay into the escrow account each month.

In addition, in jurisdictions that levy a real estate property transfer tax, a transfer tax declaration is required. The loan amount, interest rate, payment due dates, loan period, and where payments should be received will all be included in the note. They could also contain details about an ARM loan, a balloon loan, assumption clauses, and prepayment penalties. An assumption provision allows the loan to be assumed by a new buyer. Every year after closing, borrowers should get an Escrow Analysis Statement detailing the receipts and disbursements for taxes and insurance for the previous year. The lender may owe the borrower a refund within 30 days if they paid more than was required. If the borrower did not pay enough, they may be required to pay the balance within 30 days or split it over the next 12 months if they did not pay enough.

Funding

Borrowers who receive a Notice of Right to Rescind have three business days, including Saturdays, to cancel their loan after it closes. The majority of the time, financing does not occur until the rescission period has expired. Borrower and lender funds are usually required for loans. Borrowers must have enough money to cover the down payment and closing expenses, while lenders must be able to fund the loan. For closing costs, lenders prefer documented/seasoned funds, which the borrower usually sends to the closing agent's account.

Checking and savings accounts, vested retirement funds, trust accounts, equities, bonds, mutual funds, and personal gifts that match specific criteria are all common sources of funds. If the borrower wants to use funds from a previous house sale, they must present a copy of the closing statement from that transaction to the lender. The utilization of "sweat" equity and cash-on-hand for fundraising is often prohibited.

Direct investor money, table funding, and warehouse funding are all options for the lender. When a lender advances a loan directly, there are no middlemen involved. The term "table funding" refers to a transaction in which one party (the broker) closes a residential mortgage loan in their name using funds provided by a third party (the lender). However, the loan is assigned to the lender at the time of settlement, and the lender advances the funds for the loan simultaneously. When a lender uses a commercial bank's line of credit to make a loan, the bank maintains the mortgage and note as collateral for a short time before selling them to a long-term investor.

CHAPTER FOUR
UNIFORM STATE CONTENT

SAFE Act

This is the secure and fair enforcement for the mortgage licensing Act that was enacted on the 30th of July, 2008. It requires that anyone who wants to work as an MLO be state-licensed or federally licensed.

Just like state licensing. Federal licensing is also done through the NMLS website and is only available to employees of;

- A depository institution (includes credit unions)
- A subsidiary regulated by any federal bank agency and also any entity controlled and owned by any depository institution.
- Any institution regulated under the Farm Credit Administration.

Once an MLO starts the process of federal registration, they are given a unique identification number which may sometimes be required to be presented to customers.

As an employer of a federally registered MLO, you will be required to adopt the written policies and procedures compliant with the SAFE Act and its implementing regulation called "regulation G." You will also have independent testing of the policies and procedures every year.

Any federally-licensed MLO must provide the following to the registry;

• Personal identification details such as their name, date of birth, gender, social security number, home address, etc.

• Proof of employment history in finance-related services prior to ten years.

• Disclose any criminal, judicial, civil, foreign, state, or federal financial authority regulations actions taken against the MLO.

• Fingerprints for the background conducted by the Federal Bureau of Investigation.

Once the MLO has submitted all this information, they must authorize the registry to make some of the information public.

There is a two-month renewal period every year where all registered MLO's are required to renew their registration. Any individual that does not renew will have their license considered inactive and cannot act as an MLO. The only individuals exempted from this are those who completed their initial registration fewer than six months before the renewal period.

Purposes of the Safe Act

1. Ensure uniformity in license applications and the reporting requirements for all state-licensed MLO's.

2. Provide a supervisory database and comprehensive licensing.

3. Improves how information flows between regulators.

4. Reduces the burden of regulation by streamlining the process of licensing.

5. Supports measures against fraud and enhances the protection of consumers.

6. Ensure information about MLO's is accessible to consumers for free

7. Provides comprehensive training to ensure responsible behavior in the mortgage market.

• • •

State Mortgage Regulatory Agencies

To ensure that mortgage companies are acting accordingly, the federal government supervises them through several agencies and Acts by =Congress. Some of the main Acts enforced by Congress include;

- ECOA (Equal Credit Opportunity Act) – Ensures that everyone gets a fair chance at getting a mortgage despite their credit history.
- TILA (Truth in Lending Act) – Protects customers from fraudulent credit card practices.
- RESPA (Real Estate Settlement Procedures Act) – Requires lenders to give borrowers timely disclosures regarding the costs of the settlement process.

There are so many Acts put in place by Congress to regulate the practices of these mortgage companies, but there are also government agencies that include;

- CFCB (Consumer Financial Protection Bureau) – This is the main enforcer of the laws protecting consumers from unfairness in the mortgage market.
- HUD (Department of Housing and Development) – Enforces the Fair Housing Act. It protects consumers against discrimination when renting or buying a home.

• FTC (Federal Trade Commission) – Regulates against deceptive practices against consumers, such as omitting important information or charging questionable fees.

The federal register has a code of federal regulations that implement consumer protection laws, and it is updated once every year. These regulations include;

- Regulation B (Equal Opportunity Act) – Ensures that everybody can apply for the mortgage without being discriminated against on the basis of gender, race, religion, age, etc.

- Regulation C (Home Mortgage Disclosure) – Ensures that certain loan data is disclosed to the public, which will show institutional lending patterns.

- Regulation D (Alternative Mortgage Transaction Parity) – It balances consumers' access to responsible credit.

- Regulation E (Electronic Fund Transfers) – It protects individuals using these transfer services from being taken advantage of.

- Regulation F (Fair Debt Collection Practices Act) – Ensures debt collectors do not use abusive means on customers.

- Regulation G (SAFE Mortgage Licensing Act – Federal Registration of Residential Mortgage Loan Originators) – Holds mortgage loan originators accountable and protects customers from mortgage fraud.

- Regulation H (SAFE Mortgage Licensing Act – State Bureau and compliance Registration System) – Ensure minimum uniform standards are adopted for licensing and registering residential mortgage loan originators.

- Regulation I (Disclosure Requirements for Depository Institutions Lacking Federal Deposit Insurance) – Requires depository institutions to disclose some insurance-related information in account records and locations where deposits are received.

- Regulation J (Land Registration) – Provides guidelines on selling or leasing any land lots.

- Regulation K (Purchasers Revocation Rights, Sales Practises and Standards) – This provides the appropriate measure to take when a purchaser no longer wants to buy the property in question.

- Regulation L (Special Rules of Practice) – Refers to the procedure developers must undertake when correcting their record statements.

- Regulation M (Consumer Leasing) – Defines the terms involved when individuals lease their personal property.

- Regulation N (Mortgage Acts and Practices-Advertising) – It outlines all the violations that should be avoided when dealing with credit mortgage products.

- Regulation O (Mortgage Assistance Relief Services) – This refers to a program offered to consumers to assist them with any queries regarding their mortgage.

- Regulation P (Privacy of Consumer Financial Information) – Ensures that any confidential information about consumers stays private.

- Regulation V (Fair Credit Reporting) – Ensures that those determining a consumer's credit eligibility stay fair.

- Regulation X (Real Estate Settlement Procedures Act) – This refers to the financial information required when dealing with a federally related mortgage loan.

- Regulation Z (Truth in Lending) – Ensures that consumers receive more information about the real estate settlement they are working on.

- Regulation DD (Truth in Savings) – It requires depository institutions to provide certain disclosures so that customers can compare institutions and make an informed decision.

All these regulations are designed to protect consumers and lenders so that they all legally benefit from one another.

These regulatory powers combined all have certain responsibilities to consumers that they must live up to, which include;

• Issuing licenses to qualified Mortgage Loan Originators.

• Writing down the necessary procedures to be followed.

• Conducting investigations and examining individuals involved in any actions against the mortgage laws.

• Revoking or suspending licenses of any MLO displaying irresponsibility at work.

The NMLS Registry

The NMLS databse was established by the American Association of Residential Mortgage Regulators (AARMR) and the Conference of State Bank Supervisors (CSBS). It began operating in January 2008, and its responsibility is to;

i. Reduce Regulatory burden

ii. Reduce Fraud

iii. Increase uniformity

iv. Protect consumers

An MLO must register in the NMLS registry in order to get gainful employment, and it is the employer's duty to make sure that every MLO who they employ has a unique identifier obtained from the registry.

If an MLO ceases to be an employee, the institution must notify the registry within 30 days so that it can be made public to consumers that the loan originator is no longer associated with said institution.

When a covered financial institution registers one or more Mortgage loan originators, it must submit the following to the NMLS registry;

- Their contact information
- The Employer Tax Identification Number
- The RSSD (Research Statistics Supervision and Discounts) number that was issued by the board.
- The Primary Federal Regulator
- The Primary Contact for the Registry
- The individuals authorized to update information in the registry
- If it is a subsidiary, it must show that and provide the RSSD number of the parent institution.

These institutions must follow the policies and procedures set by the SAFE Act. These policies require the institution to;

- Ensure all the MLO's under their employment have met all the registry requirements.
- Establish a procedure to make sure all the policies of the SAFE Act are met.

• Create tracking systems to monitor their MLO's

• Provide appropriate actions against employees who fail to comply with the policies.

• Establish the process to be followed when reviewing an employee's criminal background.

• Ensure any third party it might be in business with complies with the SAFE Act.

• Provide annual independent testing of its personnel.

Education Requirements

Continuing education requirements are set in place to ensure that an MLO stays qualified to provide the best service to consumers. There is a total of 8 hours of education which is approved by the NMLS.

These 8 hours of education include;

- 3 hours studying federal law and regulations

- 3 hours of ethics (involves consumer protection policies)

- 2 hours of training in lending standards associated with non-traditional mortgage products.

MLO's are required to meet these requirements every year, otherwise they risk having their licenses revoked. Examinations are required for the covered financial institutions too.

These examinations are done for several purposes, which include;

- Determining if the institution complies with the SAFE Act regulations.

- To find out if the institutions have been doing their annual independent testing.

- Determining if institutions have policies in place to ensure the SAFE Act is upheld.

- To find out if customers are being provided with the unique identifiers of the MLO's.

- To determine if the shortcomings identified in the independent testing were rectified.

A set procedure is followed when doing this examination, involving the following steps;

1. Scoping (This is done to find out if the institution or its subsidiary has employed any MLO's)

2. Policies and Procedures

Determines whether the institution has adopted the policies of the SAFE Act. The minimum requirements include;

- Identifying the MLO's in the institution

- All the MLO'S must be instructed on how to comply with the SAFE Act

- Create procedures to ensure compliance with the unique identifier requirements.

- Establish procedures to ensure employee registrations are accurate.

- Establish systems that ensure that annual independent testing is done.

- Provide necessary actions to be taken against employees who do not comply with the policies.

3. Using the Unique Identifier

Find out if the institution avails their MLO's unique identifiers to their customers. This can be done either;

- Upon request (written or oral)

- Prior to acting as an MLO

- Through any initial document passed between the MLO and the customer

4. Record Keeping

Ensuring that these covered institutions have sufficient records proving that they have complied with the SAFE Act. These records may include registration requirements, criminal background checks, and proof that the MLO's have been using their unique identifiers.

MLO Unique Identifiers are a series of numbers an MLO receives after registering in the NMLS registry.

They will use this number forever, and it can never be the same as somebody elses number.

These unique identifiers serve to;

- Help track MLO's between states or when they change employers.

- Help customers validate if the MLO they are working with is legitimate.

Apart from personal information, any other detail regarding an MLO's work ethic and information is publicly available on the NMLS website, and customers can access it whenever they please.

MLO's are required to give customers their unique identifier before commencing any transactions. The institution can also do this by;

- Providing a list of registered MLO's in their employ and their unique identifiers on their website.

- Posting the information in a public place within its premises such as the lobby or the reception area.

- Create a system where other employees can provide these unique identifiers when customers ask for them instead of waiting for the MLO to provide them.

The CFPB Authority

This is the Consumer Protection Bureau that supervises banks, lenders, and some other large non-bank institutions like debt collection companies and credit reporting agencies. The CFPB enforces federal consumer financial laws to make sure that all consumers have access to fair and transparent financial products. Generally speaking, the CFPB serves to protect the rights of consumers, which include:

- The Right to be Informed – As a consumer, you deserve accurate information so you can make a good decision. For example, businesses must show all the components in their financial products upfront.

- Right to choose – Several businesses may be offering the product you want, but you are free to choose the one you feel best suits your needs.

- Right to safety – Manufacturers, for example, have a legal responsibility to provide you with products that are safe to use. This is why the US Consumer Product Safety Commission exists, to enforce these safety standards.

- Right to be heard – If you have a complaint about any product, the people that sold it to you are obligated to listen to you and fix the issue.

- Right to consumer education – You deserve to know how a market works so you can get the best value for your money. You should know how to compare offers and get the best products available.

• Right to service – You are entitled to be treated with the utmost respect no matter the good or service you are in the market for. You should be able to do buinsess without discrimination of gender, age, race, and so on and so on.

Apart from safeguarding consumers' rights, the CFPB has other roles, which include;

• Making rules that govern consumer finance markets and making the existing ones more effective

• Inviting the public to share their views about various documents and proposed rules.

• Encouraging competition and innovation

• Convenes advisory committees to provide input on policies, consumer engagement, research, etc.

• Ensure customers have a variety of financial products to choose from through working with community banks and credit unions.

THE LOAN ORIGINATOR'S RULE

This rule prohibits compensation that is based on loan terms instead of the loan amount. It falls under the Truth in Lending Act of Regulation Z.

The rule has three separate compliances to follow;

- June 1st, 2013 - Prohibits waiver of certain federal rights in open and closed-end loans.

- January 1st, 2014 - Establishing requirements that define compensation and qualification of an MLO.

- January 10th, 2014 - Prohibiting financing credit insurance on any loan applications after this date.

The CFPB adopted this rule to implement the Dodd-Frank Act loan originator provisions. Other provisions adopted under this rule include;

• Financing credit insurance premiums was restricted.

• Mandatory identifying of all the information on loan documents.

• Provides clear policies and procedures to make sure the rule is followed.

• Prohibits waivers on federal claims available to the customers.

The rule also gives a very clear definition of a loan originator. It says that a loan originator is a person or institution that expects compensation directly or indirectly after performing any of the following duties;

- Assisting a customer to apply or get credit.

- Negotiating credit extension for another person.

- Performing loan origination services.

LICENSE LAWS AND REGULATIONS

Any individual interested in becoming a mortgage loan originator must be licensed by the NMLS. For this to be achieved, you must do the following;

• Register on the NMLS website where you will get a unique identifier.

• Complete 20 hours of mandatory education courses

• Take an exam and get a score of 75% and above.

• If you pass, submit the necessary documents to the NMLS system, then wait.

The application process once you have passed the exam is not complicated. It involves the following steps;

• Submitting your application on the NMLS website

• Submitting fingerprints for a background check by the FBI

• Authorizing a credit report

• Providing any supporting documents requested

• Have your employer submit your company sponsorship request. If you are not employed then your license will be issued as inactive. You can update this on the website when you get employed.

To get your MLO license, you must meet the following NMLS requirements;

• Complete the pre-licensing 20-hour education requirement

• Be above 18 years old

• Pass the written test

• Have an NMLS account with all your details filled in and all the necessary documents submitted.

However, there are a few mishaps that may cause you to be denied a license, or to have an existing one revoked. Examples of these mishaps include;

• Having ever had your license revoked in the past.

• If you have ever been convicted of a crime that involves financial dishonesty - such as fraud.

• If you did not meet the pre-licensing educational requirement.

• If you are proved to be financially irresponsible, such as having a really low credit score.

NMLS Temporary Authority

This rule allows a qualified MLO applicant to act as a loan originator while they are still going through the licensing process. It is available to federally registered MLOs who are changing employment to a state-registered company. It also applies to MLOs that are already state-registered but want to seek licenses in other states. It is important to know that the temporary authority only covers the duties of a loan originator, so if additional activities are part of your license, you will not be in a position to do them until your license is finalized.

To qualify for this temporary authority;

- The company the MLO works for must be licensed in the application state.
- The company must prove the MLO is a W-2 employee
- The company has to sponsor the MLO in the NMLS system.
- The MLO must have been registered federally one year prior to the application date.
- The MLO must have been state-licensed continuously for 30 days prior to the application date.

COMPLIANCE

Mortgage compliances are the rules and regulations controlling the mortgage process.

The most important step in compliance is understanding whether your loan falls under RESPA (Real Estate Settlement Procedures Act) or TILA (Truth in

Lending Act). These two combined impose regulations such as;

• HOEPA (Home Ownership and Equity Protection Act) – Protects homeowners from overpaying the Private Mortgage Insurance (PMI). This is generally paid by buyers who pay a 20% or less down-payment.

• ATR/QM (Ability to Pay/Qualified Mortgage) Rule – This one makes it much harder for lenders to give loans that do not serve the borrower's best interests. It requires good faith determination regarding the borrower's ability to pay.

• LO Comp (Loan Originator Compensation) Rule – It ensures that any compensation paid is based on the loan amount and not the terms of the contract or other proxies.

• TRID (TILA RESPA Integrated Disclosure) – It changes the timelines of some mortgage processes. It also provides more clarity to consumers about the costs involved in getting the mortgage.

TILA

The Truth in Lending Act protects customers from credit card discrepancies. It requires the lender to give consumers all the information they need about the loan to do comparison shopping. Such information involves the terms of the loan, the annual percentage rates, and the total costs to be incurred.

RESPA

The Real Estate Settlement Procedures Act restricts how ESCROW accounts are used and eliminates any abusive practices during settlement. It also ensures that sellers and buyers have disclosures on the total settlement costs.

FHA

The Fair Housing Act applies to those who engage in residential real estate. It allows for this kind of property to be appraised and sold.

ECOA

The Equal Credit Opportunities Act prohibits any discrimination against lenders or borrowers based on gender, race, religion, age, etc. It ensures that everyone gets an equal shot at applying for credit.

FCRA

The Fair Credit Reporting Act imposes adverse action and requirements on anyone that uses consumer reports. Lenders are advised to be careful not to use these reports with any commercial transactions.

Flood Insurance

This Act discourages homeowners from living in areas that are prone to floods. Purchasing this insurance protects the property in case of any damage caused when it floods. The location of the property and the type of collateral will determine how these insurance laws will apply.

SAFE Act

The Secure and Fair Enforcement for Mortgage Licensing Act protects consumers by holding lenders accountable. It requires MLO's to register with the NMLS system and to renew this registration annually to ensure they still meet the minimum qualifications. This ensures that consumers are getting the best services possible.

EFTA

The Electronic Funds Transfer Act protects customers transferring funds through electronic means such as ATMs, debit cards, point-of-sale terminals, and so on. It allows users to correct any transaction errors and limits any liabilities arising from stolen or lost cards.

If you are enjoying utilizing this book in your studies, please leave us a 5* review on Amazon or Audible, whichever you used to get the book or audiobook. It helps more than you could ever know!

CHAPTER FIVE

BASIC FINANCIAL CALCULATIONS

PERIODIC INTEREST

Periodic interest refers to interest earned over a set period of time. The interest rate on a mortgage is usually mentioned annually, however, the interest rate is compounded more frequently (usually on a monthly basis). The first payment is generally not due for at least a month after a loan closes. For example, if a loan closes on May 20th, the first payment isn't due until July 1st. Because mortgage interest is paid in arrears, the July interest payment will include interest from June, while the principal payment will only cover July. Because most of a loan's first few years are spent on interest, the lender deems a missed month of principal payments (in this case, June) insignificant. The interest charged on a daily basis is known as "per diem interest." Most mortgage lenders will charge borrowers interest on a loan from the closing date through the end of the month. For example, if a borrower ends their loan on May 20th, they will pay interest on the loan from May 20th to May 31st, inclusive of the settlement date, for a total of 12 days of interest. The annual interest amount is computed by multiplying the loan amount by the annual interest rate to get the per diem interest. Per diem interest is calculated by dividing the annual interest amount by 365 days. So, if a borrower closes on a loan on May 20th with a loan amount of $100,000 and an annual interest rate of 7%, the $100,000 loan amount is multiplied by the 7% annual interest rate to get $7,000 in yearly interest. The $7,000 in annual interest is then divided by 365 to generate $19.18 in per diem interest. Because May has 31 days and the loan completed on the 20th, we would multiply $19.18 by the remaining 12 days in May (including the day of closure) to get the total per diem interest of $230.16, which the borrower pays at closing. Further examples of these calculations can be found in the questions and answers section in Chapter 8.

PAYMENTS

The cost of mortgage insurance is determined by the loan amount. Mortgage insurance typically costs 0.5 to 1.5 percent of the loan amount per year. A $250,000 loan with a 1% mortgage insurance factor, for example, would cost $2,500 per year. If the premium is paid in advance, it will be included in the closing fees.

Borrowers can alternatively pay their premiums monthly, which means dividing the annual cost by 12 and adding it to their monthly mortgage payment. In this scenario, the monthly insurance premiums for the borrower would be $2,500 divided by 12 months, or equivalent to $208.33 per month. This sum would be collected and stored in an escrow account until the mortgage insurance premium was due. Lenders can use the interest formula Rate = I/P*t to determine interest rates, where I is the amount of interest paid in a given time period, P is the principal amount, t is the time period, and Rate (r) is the interest rate in decimal form. Principal and interest, as well as any escrow monies collected by the lender for bills such as property tax or insurance, are included in monthly payments. The monthly mortgage payment is computed by adding the principle and interest to any escrow funds monthly installments. For example, if a $250,000 loan had a monthly principal and interest payment of $600, monthly hazard insurance of $100, monthly property taxes of $166.67, and a monthly mortgage insurance premium of $104.17, the total monthly payment would be $970.84. If any of the bills kept in escrow increase or decrease, the borrower's monthly payment will increase or decrease as well. So, with I = $970.84, P = $250,000 and t = 12 months, then Rate = 5.83%.

DOWN PAYMENT

The loan amount plus the down payment equals the purchasing price of a home. Typically, down payments are expressed as a percentage of the purchase price. For example, a down payment of $8,750 on a $250,000 home is stated as a 3.5 percent down payment. The percentage amount is derived by dividing the down payment amount by the purchase price and multiplying the decimal figure by 100.

RATIOS OF LOAN-TO-VALUE

The loan-to-value ratio, or LTV, is a calculation that compares the loan amount to the market value of the collateral. It is computed by dividing the loan amount by the purchase price or appraised value of the home, whichever is lower. Furthermore, the purchase price is equal to the loan amount plus the down payment, and the owner's equity is equal to the market value minus the loan balance. If a residence has multiple mortgages, the combined loan-to-value ratio, or CLTV, is computed by putting all of the loan amounts together and dividing by the lower of the purchase price or appraised current value of the home. A home with a purchase price of $100,000 and a loan amount of $80,000, for example, has an LTV of 80%, while a home with a purchase price of $100,000 and loan amounts of $80,000 and $10,000 has a CLTV of 90%.

DEBT-TO-INCOME RATIOS

The PITI payment for the possible loan is added to the borrower's other monthly debt and divided by the borrower's gross monthly income to compute the debt-to-income ratio. For example, if a borrower has a $200 monthly loan and a $1,400 PITI payment, the total debt would be $1,600. The debt-to-income ratio is 32 percent if the borrower's gross monthly income is $5,000. Credit card payments, lease payments, alimony, child support, and other monthly recurring debt are all included in the debt-to-income ratio. For loans that are manually underwritten, Fannie Mae requires a maximum total debt-to-income ratio of 36 percent (up to 45 percent if the borrower achieves the good credit and reserve requirements reflected in the approval matrix) and a maximum debt-to-income ratio of 50 percent for loans underwritten by Desktop Underwriter. FHA loans have a maximum debt-to-income ratio of 43%, whereas VA loans have a maximum debt-to-income ratio of 41%. Qualified Mortgages have a maximum loan-to-value ratio of 43%.

INTEREST RATE BUY-DOWNS: DISCOUNT POINT

The interest rate on a permanent note is set by the borrower and is used to compute the monthly principal and interest payments. A discount point is a fee paid by the borrower in exchange for a lower interest rate. Loan originators consult the lender's rate charts, which show the available range of interest rates as well as the cost of buying down to a lower rate. The borrower is responsible for paying discount points as a closing cost. One percent of the loan amount is equal to one discount point. One discount point on a $100,000 loan, for example, would cost the borrower $1,000. Whether paying the discount points is worthwhile for the borrower is determined by factors such as how long they plan to keep the property or how long it will take for the savings to be reconciled after paying the discount points at closing.

PREPAID ITEMS AND CLOSING COSTS

The down payment, attorney's fees, deed recording fees, property survey, financing fee, upfront mortgage insurance premiums, per diem interest, escrow money for insurance and property taxes, or loan origination fees - could all be included in the buyer's closing expenses. Because the first payment isn't due until the following month, the escrow costs will include funds due the month after closing. Any unpaid loan balances and prorated mortgage interest for the days they hold the property could be included in the seller's closing fees (excluding the day of closing, which is the buyer's responsibility). Lenders typically ask borrowers to pay their insurance policies in full at closing or in monthly payments that are added to their monthly payment.

The policies must be in effect on the day of closing in any case. Lenders may still require the borrower to pay a year in advance at closing for refinances with existing insurance coverage. Simply add together the monthly payments for each month of the current year policy plus two months of buffer to calculate the amount owed. If the policy began in July and the refinance is scheduled to close in September, you add the monthly payments for August, September, plus two months of cushion. Add seven months of monthly payments (August - February) + two months of buffer if the refinance closes in February. RESPA also authorizes the lender to charge an extra two months of escrow payments at closing to ensure that bills are paid if the borrower falls behind on their payments.

ADJUSTABLE RATE MORTGAGES (ARMS)

These are rates that can be changed as mortgage interest rates fluctuate, and they are computed by adding the index rate and the margin (together, they are known as the fully indexed rate). The index rate is a variable rate based on a financial indicator like the US Treasury Securities rate or LIBOR, whereas the margin rate is a fixed rate that includes the lender's profit and overhead. During the loan's adjustment period, the index rate may vary. If the loan has a one-year adjustment period, for example, the index rate can change once a year. When the adjustment period ends, the new interest rate must be determined by multiplying the margin by the current index rate. If the current index rate is 1.2 percent and the margin is 2.5 percent, the fully indexed rate for the next 12 months will be 3.7 percent. However, if the index rate rises to 1.4 percent during the next adjustment period, the new fully indexed rate will fall to 3.9 percent for the next 12 months. The borrower's monthly mortgage payment will be affected by these modifications. For example, if the annual interest rate on a $100,000 loan is 3.7 percent, the monthly interest payment would be $308.33. The new monthly interest rate would be $325.00 if the interest rate increased to 3.9 percent per year due to varying economic conditions.

CHAPTER SIX

ETHICS/FRAUD

The moral principles that guide an individual's behavior and conduct are referred to as ethics. You are working for the borrower as a Mortgage Loan Originator (MLO), but you also have a responsibility to safeguard your company's brand and reputation. Ignoring ethics not only harms your reputation, but can also get you in legal trouble.

As previously said, everyone has the right to apply for a mortgage and receive the best available help. That being said, you must act honestly and cannot falsify any information on documents in order to benefit your client. All things have to be done in a fair manner. Mortgage fraud can be committed by intentionally providing inaccurate information on an application.

You are not allowed to engage in redlining, which is the practice of refusing to accept an application based on the location of a property. In addition, reverse redlining is disallowed, which involves stigmatizing a neighborhood based on various risk characteristics and charging higher interest rates and costs to acquire a mortgage. Furthermore, a client can't be persuaded to live in a given location or to use a specific loan program. You must inform your client of all the options available to them. You can teach them everything, but that's about it.

There must be no potential for a conflict of interest. If an appraiser is connected to somebody on the loan, for example, they must be replaced right away. It is your job as an originator to report any inaccurate information provided by your client to a compliance officer, or you may be fined. You must also make certain that the underwriter has the necessary information. If you suppress information which is discovered later, the corporation may be forced to buy the loan, which will fall back on you. Your files will be inspected, which isn't something you would want to happen.

Essentially, you want to act in a trustworthy and honest manner. It is preferable to find out rather than assume if you are unclear about something. Keep in mind that your business, your routine, and even your freedom are all on the line. In the following portions of this chapter, we'll go through more particular ethical difficulties in detail.

VIOLATIONS OF LAW

The Gramm-Leach-Bliley Act (GLBA) establishes the distinction between customers and consumers. Under the Gramm-Leach-Bliley Act, all customers are consumers, but not all consumers are customers. Banks, mortgage brokers, lenders, tax preparers, and debt collectors are all subject to the law since they provide either loans or financial advice. A consumer, as previously stated, is an individual who utilizes a financial organization's derivative or service for personal, family, or household purpose - whereas a customer is a subtype of customers who have a continuing relationship with the institution. The Financial Privacy Rule, Pretexting Rule, and Safeguards Rule are all part of the Gramm-Leach-Bliley Act.

Customers must receive a Privacy Notice and the option to opt-out of information sharing once a year, however they will only receive one if their information is shared with an affiliated organization, according to the rule. The Safeguards Rule compels financial institutions to develop procedures to help secure an individual's private information, while Pre-Texting prevents financial institutions from acquiring personal information under false pretenses. Financial institutions that violate the Gramm-Leach-Bliley Act face fines of up to $100,000 for each infraction, as well as fines of up to $10,000 for its officials and directors. Some may face a maximum sentence of five years in prison or a combination of prison and fines.

Prohibited Acts

Redlining is the practice of rejecting a creditworthy applicant for a home loan who lives in a specific neighborhood, even if the person is otherwise qualified.

Redlining can also be done by selectively boosting costs for applicants in a specific neighborhood. The Fair Housing Act of 1968 made it illegal to discriminate based on race, religion, national origin, sex, handicap, or familial position when selling, renting, or financing a home. Kickbacks and unearned referral fees are also illegal in the mortgage sector. The Real Estate Settlement Procedures Act prohibits anybody from paying or receiving a fee, kickback, or anything of value just for referring services to an individual or organization. When a mortgage firm compensates the real estate agents of a real estate company who refer the most business to them, this is an example of a kickback between related organizations. Real estate agents are not entitled to earn compensation because they do not genuinely deliver mortgage-related services. Another example is when a title company joins forces with a real estate company and pays them a percentage of the earnings in exchange for bringing in new business for the title company. As a result, nothing of value can be given for business recommendations from a company that is involved in or provides a settlement service for a federally connected mortgage loan. Referral fees between real estate brokerages are, however, authorized in real estate transactions. When one real estate agent suggests a customer to another real estate agent with the understanding that they will receive a share of the commission for dealing with that client, this is known as a referral. For instance, if a real estate agent exclusively works with residential properties and refers a customer wishing to buy a commercial property to another real estate agent, the referral fee is allowed. Other forbidden acts include, for example, loan processors who are permitted to execute specific functions, such as collecting, obtaining, and analyzing information relating to a mortgage loan, but are not permitted to offer or negotiate any mortgage loan conditions.

FAIRNESS IN LENDING

Coercion is a sort of predatory lending that involves using force or threats to induce someone to do something. Orally, in writing, or through other modes of communication. Due to their race, color, religion, sex, handicap, familial position, or national origin - coercion may prohibit or limit an individual's access to the sale or renting of a dwelling or other real-estate related transactions. Throughout the mortgage process, each appraiser might value a property differently than the next, but they must adhere to certain laws and principles. Regardless, some appraisers collaborate with other service providers to inflate the value of a property through illicit activity. Following the introduction of the Home Valuation Code of Conduct for single-family mortgages, mortgage brokers were no longer allowed to select the appraiser for a specific transaction. These rules were expanded to all mortgages in 2010 by the Dodd-Frank Act, even if they were not sold to Fannie Mae. The Uniform Standards of Professional Appraisal Practice, which contains rules and regulations such as the Ethics Rule, must be agreed to by appraisers. Appraiser conduct, management, secrecy, and record-keeping are all covered by the Ethics Rule. Appraisers must make certain that their reports are unbiased, non-discriminatory, and error-free. If the appraiser has valued a property in the last three years, they must provide that information in the report (unless the previous client instructed them not to disclose this, in which case they cannot value the property again). Appraisers must also state that they are paid for their work, but they are not required to reveal how much they are paid. The value of a property cannot be used to determine the compensation.

Without permission, appraisers cannot produce misleading ads or sign for another appraiser. Except for the client, client-authorized individuals, state regulatory bodies, and peer review committees, client information and appraisal report information must be kept confidential. An appraiser must preserve a file with the client's name, authorized users, copies of client reports, transcripts of oral reports, and supporting documents before submitting an appraisal report. This file must be retained for a minimum of five years and for at least two years after an appraiser is called to testify in court.

The Equal Credit Opportunity Act prohibits loan originators from discriminating against people based on their race, color, religion, national origin, sex, marital status, age, or the fact that they receive public assistance. Loan originators are not allowed to inquire about a person's religion or the number of children they want to have. Protected classes, assessment criteria, and adverse action notices are among the primary aspects of the Equal Credit Opportunity Act. Some of the protected classifications include race, color, ethnicity, religion, national origin, gender, sex, marital status, age, and receipt of public assistance. Lenders must transmit a copy of the appraisal report to the borrower at least three business days before closing. In addition, within 30 days of receiving an application, the lender must notify the applicant of the lender's decision. Within 60 days of receiving an adverse action notification, the petitioner has the legal right to request the basis for the adverse action, and the lender has 30 days to supply the requested information. It is required that all applications receive the same level of consideration.

Don't Become a Victim

The greatest method to avoid becoming a victim is to educate yourself on what's going on and to understand your rights. A borrower has the right to know what is going on with their loan application and why they were denied. They also have the right to know how their interest rate is calculated and where their fees originate from.

All people who intend to apply for a mortgage loan must be accepted by the lender. The lender must additionally provide the following documentation to the applicant at no cost:

- Estimate in Good Faith
- Statement of Truth in Lending Disclosure
- A copy of the application for a loan
- Disclosure statement for mortgage servicing
- Borrowers are also entitled to the following papers in addition to these

The Real Estate Settlement Services Special Information Booklet includes information about real estate settlement services. This information is only needed when a borrower is actually buying a house, not simply considering it.

When a loan is closed or resolved, a HUD-1 settlement statement is issued. Borrowers can also obtain this document one day before the closing date so that they can compare the mortgage loan costs to the Good Faith Estimate. All real estate transactions, including acquisitions, refinances, loans for property improvements, reverse mortgages, and home equity lines of credit, will result in a HUD-1 being issued to the borrower..

- All settlement expenses for all mortgage loan transactions must be disclosed in the HUD-1.
- It should detail all expenditures associated with closing that are paid either at settlement or outside of the settlement.
- During the closure or settlement, the HUD-1 must be given to the borrower.
- For conventional, FHA, and VA loans, a certificate is required.

A borrower has the option of filing a complaint with the department of housing and urban development (HUD), or a fair housing organization. This can be accomplished by calling the National Discrimination Hotline or filling out a form on the HUD website. A complaint can be filed by anyone who believes they have been the victim of lending discrimination.

A complaint will either be assigned to the Office of Fair Housing and Equal Opportunity, or FHEO, for investigation; or forwarded to a local fair housing agency once it is submitted. When a complaint is received by a fair housing office, the applicant will be notified. Throughout the inquiry, the FHEO will make every effort to seek a voluntary conclusion that benefits all parties concerned. This can lead to a conciliation agreement, which everyone must agree to. The inquiry will come to a finish at this point, and the matter will be closed by the relevant agency.

The probe will continue if the conciliation procedure fails, and it can possibly wind up in court. The applicant will not be required to pay for a lawyer if this occurs. The matter can be heard in front of an administrative hearing or a court of law if HUD or a fair lending agency finds reasonable cause for discrimination. The matter will be handled by a government attorney at no expense to the petitioner.

If the case goes to court, HUD will submit it to the Department of Justice, which will file a lawsuit in the area where the alleged prejudice occurred. If an applicant wishes to engage an attorney other than the one assigned to them, they may do so at their own expense. If it is determined that there was discrimination, the respondent may be forced to:

- Pay compensation for losses such as embarrassment & suffering - to the petitioner.
- Alternative relief options, such as loans with no discriminatory terms, should be made available
- Pay a civil penalty to the federal government that the Federal Court Judge will determine.

- Expenses for legal counsel should be reasonable
- Review Fair Lending Practices

The Federal Deposit Insurance Corporation (FDIC) of the United States contributes to the country's financial system's stability and public confidence. The Fair Lending Scope and Conclusions Memorandum was created to establish a national standard for recording the scope and conclusions of fair lending evaluations. The goal of this memorandum was to direct the examiner's attention to the areas where fair lending discrimination was most likely to occur. Interagency examinations are conducted to discover which agency may be responsible for prejudice, if any occurs.

The FLSC will assist in documenting the fair lending risks that exist, the controls for risk management that an agency has implemented, why specific focal points were chosen, the depth to which the evaluations were undertaken, as well as the findings of the study. Loan products, decision centers, marketplaces, time frames, and control groups are all included in the scope of the investigation. Examiners should concentrate their reviews on the areas that we will discuss later.

Understanding Credit Operations

Before examining for discriminatory practices, an examiner should thoroughly study information about the institution and its market to gain a detailed understanding of credit operations and the representation of prohibited basis group residents in the institution's marketplace. Before assessing if risk factors are present, examiners should gather a high level of detail. The following is some relevant background information:

- The different sorts of credit products available and their terms.
- Is there a unique credit option tailored for underserved people at the institution?
- The amount of money lent for each credit choice, as well as the rate of increase.
- The demography of the markets in which the institution conducts business. Is the market in a location where a certain race or religion has a stronghold?
- The structure of the decision-making process; this involves the delegation of different lending authority and the degree to which managers, employees, and independent brokers have price and credit term discretion.
- What is the institution's remuneration plan for loan officers and brokers?
- For lending products, any form of relevant documentation is available. Also, how accessible is this information, and how much of it is there?

- The extent to which information requests can be arranged and coordinated with other aspects of the examination; examiners should only request the information they require to complete their jobs.

When it comes to knowing a financial institution's lending operations, it's also important to be aware of any business dealings with connected or unaffiliated mortgage brokers or third-party lenders. Examiners should only select as many marketplaces as they can reasonably handle to conduct full assessments if an institution is vast and covers a wide demographic region - such as rural towns and urban areas.

Evaluating Potential Discriminatory Conduct

Based on their knowledge of credit operations, an examiner must assess the amount of information needed for the scoping procedure. There is no way to examine every possible concern that may arise in a reasonable amount of time. The following aspects should be considered when choosing products for a scoping review:

- Which products and/or forbidden items were examined at the most recent examination, and which ones were not?

- Which items and base categories are the most available in the institution's marketplace?
- Which items and forbidden base groups were investigated by the institution utilizing either a voluntarily reported self-test or a self-evaluation.

Examiners should undertake preliminary interviews with the institution's underwriting professionals, as well as with those who establish the organization's pricing policies and procedures, if possible. The examiner should evaluate the following using these interviews and the material gathered during the preceding steps:

- The underwriting policies, methods, and recommendations.
- The credit score methodology, described in detail. This comprises a list of scoring factors, cutoff scores, the scope of validation, and any overrides and exceptions policies.
- Loan application forms.
- Any appropriate pricing rules, risk-based policies, and instructions for exercising loan terms discretion.
- Relationships between the institution and other financial institutions.
- The databases for lending products that are used and maintained.

- Documents that outline policy exceptions or overrides, reporting exceptions, and how it's all kept track of.
- Copies of any consumer complaints alleging discrimination.
- Materials for compliance programs, training manuals, and organizational charts.
- Copies of marketing plans that are currently available.

The next step is to identify discrimination risk factors after gaining an overview. To comprehend the many methods involved in the fair lending system, the examiner will analyze the material from the agency's work papers, institutional records, and any in-depth interviews with management representatives. Here are several red signs that indicate a high probability of prejudice at the institution:

- The record-keeping for compliance is inadequate.
- There is no required information for banned grounds monitoring, as mandated by law.
- Previous examinations were less reliable due to poor data or concerns with record keeping.
- Fair lending issues have already been discovered in one or more of the institution's products.

- The compliance management program's size, scope, and quality are all significantly lesser than those seen in similar-sized programs.
- The institution's rules and procedures have not been updated to meet new laws and regulations.
- The staff's fair lending training is either inadequate or non-existent.

Once these risk variables have been discovered, it's time to look at the residential loan products, which are where the majority of the discrimination occurs. Home mortgage loans fall into three categories: home purchases, home upgrades, and refinancing. If the institution deals with a large number of these products, these categories can be subdivided even further:

- Loans backed by the government.
- Mobile homes or other manufactured housing loans.
- Wholesale, indirect, and brokered loans are all available.
- Portfolio lending.

Examiners must also establish whether a certain institution offers low-cost housing loan programs, special-purpose credit programs, or other programs aimed at a specific set of borrowers, such as underserved communities. The examination will next proceed via the following steps:

1. Identifying characteristics that cause prejudice in residential lending.
2. Organize and conduct a Residential Risk Analysis.
3. Determine the likelihood of discrimination in consumer financing.
4. Determine the likelihood of commercial lending discrimination.
5. Complete the entire scoping procedure.

The entire examination scope process is lengthy and involved, and examiners must get to the bottom of things while weighing a variety of variables before deciding whether or not specific activities were discriminatory. They clearly want to avoid making any false charges on either side.

FRAUD DETECTION

Mortgage fraud can be classified into two categories: property fraud and profit fraud. The intentional misrepresentation or omission of information with the goal to fool or mislead a lender into giving credit that would not be offered if the true facts were known is defined as property fraud. Homebuyers aiming to purchase homes for their own personal use are the most common perpetrators of property fraud.

Fraud for profit is frequently conducted with the help of industry insiders such as mortgage brokers, real estate agents, property appraisers, and settlement agents for monetary gain (including attorneys and title examiners). To profit from the mortgage process, several stakeholders collaborate together.

Asset fraud, occupancy fraud, income fraud, employment fraud, and liability fraud are all examples of mortgage fraud. Borrowers misrepresent assets and income through manufacturing information such as designing fake employers and fraudulent pay stubs, as well as creating or changing bank statements.

When a buyer falsifies the planned use of the property being financed, this is known as occupancy fraud. For example, a borrower claiming that the home will be their primary residence in order to qualify for cheaper interest rates when the property will be rented out. When a buyer asserts self-employment income that does not exist, misrepresents their job status, or utilizes fraudulent employment verification documents, they are committing employment fraud. A borrower who wants to conceal facts about money they owe or are due to pay is committing liability fraud. The Red Flags Rule was put in place to help identify warning indicators that could suggest fraudulent or identity theft activities in order to combat these activities. It also necessitates that some financial institutions establish procedures that instruct workers on how to spot and respond to these warning indications. Many other warning signs may be discovered through the whole mortgage process, such as the property seller not being the property owner on record, a recent quitclaim deed that transferred ownership, early payment defaults, an incomplete or illegible appraisal, an unexplained large deposit in a borrower's account, multiple outstanding loans from one person, a short sale or loan modification without proof of financial hardship, incomplete leases, and multiple changes to writability.

The following are some examples of common but simple mortgage fraud schemes:

Asset rentals - This sort of fraud occurs when a borrower temporarily deposits monies or assets from another person into their account in order to seem qualified for financing. After the mortgage is closed, the funds are returned to whoever provided them.

Fake down payments - This sort of fraud occurs when a person falsifies documents and/or the down payment verification to borrow money from another party.

Appraisal fraud - Happens when an appraiser inflates an appraisal report in order to qualify for a bigger mortgage from the lender.

Document fraud - When documents are provided to lenders with fake or altered information, this is referred to as document fraud.

Fraudulent shell firms - A shell company is used illegally to perform and disguise financial transactions in this sort of fraud.

Identity theft - Happens when a person gets and fraudulently utilizes another person's social security number, birth date, address, and other personal information in order to secure mortgage financing. Stolen pay stubs, bank documents, tax returns, W-2s, and forged employment verification letters are all examples of identity theft for mortgage reasons.

Silent seconds - When an applicant obtains funding for a down payment without informing the lender, the lien for the funds may go unregistered.

Nominee borrower - Sometimes known as straw borrowers, nominee borrowing occurs when one party pays another party with good credit to act as the borrower.

Some mortgage fraudsters find ways to pull off more intricate schemes, such as:

Air loans - When a group of criminals work together to file for a mortgage on a non-existent property or with a non-existent borrower, this sort of fraud happens. The air loan fraud simply transfers money to the culprits; no property is ever purchased or sold.

Builder bailout - This sort of fraud occurs when a builder has unsold apartments and tries to sell them using various fraudulent tactics, such as disguised down payment aid or excessive seller concessions. The naïve financial institution mortgaging the unit is often left with a loan secured by an inflated collateral value, and the "actual" loan-to-value ends up being larger than 100% as a result of the deception.

Buy and bail - This occurs when a homeowner has a mortgage balance that is greater than the home's market value (or is facing impending financial hardship that will negatively impact them), so they purchase a less expensive investment property that they intend to live in while bailing on the previous home, allowing it to go into foreclosure. In order to demonstrate their ability to cover housing bills, the buyer may even fabricate tenants and leases.

Chunking - This type of fraud occurs when a fraudulent seller acts as an agent and persuades a buyer to buy at least one investment property, then arranges multiple closings with multiple lenders for the same property in a short period of time, leaving the buyer owing multiple loans while the seller walks away with the loan proceeds. The property is left to foreclose, putting the lenders at risk of losing money. To make this technique work, you'll almost always require the help of a title business or a real estate broker. To misrepresent the acquisition of several houses, the seller may craft straw buyers or change loan documentation.

Double selling - This is a sort of fraud in which a borrower conspires with a mortgage broker to use the borrower's home as collateral for multiple home equity lines of credit from various financial institutions. To take advantage of the delay in the recording of the mortgages, the lines of credit are then closed in a short period of time. Furthermore, the mortgage broker distorts the borrower's financial facts in order to boost the borrower's debt capacity. However, if a loan originator uses a warehouse lender to offer short-term funding and subsequently sells the loan to other investors, they can occasionally complete this deception without the borrower's knowledge.

Equity skimming - This form of fraud is committed in a number of ways, but it always involves an inflated assessment and a dishonest buyer or homeowner. An appraiser may overvalue a property so that the buyer can pocket additional funds after closing, or so that the homeowner can participate in a cash-out refinance.

Fictitious loans - This sort of fraud involves fabricating loan paperwork or using a stolen identity to apply for a loan and then pocketing the proceeds. The culprit, in most cases, has no intention of repaying the debt. It can be carried out by financial institution insiders such as loan originators, real estate brokers, title companies, or appraisers.

Falsifying financial issues to qualify for lower-income loans, such as modification or refinancing, is a sort of loan modification and refinance fraud.

Mortgage servicing fraud happens when a mortgage servicer takes advantage of an opportunity to profit from a step in the mortgage servicing process, such as selling a loan they service but failing to send the proceeds to the loan's owner after the sale. The servicer continues to pay principal and interest on the loans, despite the owner being unaware that the loan has been sold.

Phantom sale - This sort of fraud occurs when someone records a fraudulent quitclaim deed on an abandoned house and either borrows money or sells it.

Property flipping fraud - There are two types of property flipping fraud. The first is when an investor makes a bid to buy a home that has been on the market for a long time for any amount above the asking price, which is then backed up by an inflated appraisal (often backed up through non-existent home improvements that were supposedly made). The seller obtains the net profits they were originally asking for at closing, plus a payback from the seller's money on the HUD-1 Settlement Statement, which goes to the fraudsters.

Secondly, individuals, businesses, or straw borrowers may commit flip fraud by buying and selling properties amongst themselves in a short timeframe in order to artificially raise the value of the properties. The goal of this technique is to extract as much money as possible from the property, and the loan proceeds are frequently used for purposes other than those specified on the application.

Reverse mortgage fraud - Happens when falsified appraisals or changed birthdates are used to raise the amount of money a person is eligible for through a reverse mortgage. The value of the home determines the maximum loan amount that borrowers can qualify for with reverse mortgages, and under the term program, in which a borrower receives equal monthly payments for a set period of time, older borrowers would receive larger payments due to a shorter payment stream, creating a direct incentive to lie about their age.

Short sale fraud - Short sale fraud happens when a buyer in a short sale deal is related to the seller or when financial documents are manipulated to reflect a financial hardship. The offender may even utilize a straw buyer and default on the loan, which they could then exploit to get a better deal on the house.

The red flags on a sales contract might encompass a wide range of concerns due to the prevalence of mortgage fraud schemes. Non-arm's-length deals in which the seller is also a real estate broker, relative, employer, or other form of interested party are some potential red flags. If the seller is not listed on the title, the purchaser is not the genuine application, or the purchaser or purchasers were erased, these are all red flags. Another red signal could be the lack of a real estate agent, the use of a power of attorney, or the presence of a second mortgage on the application that is not revealed.

In terms of money, putting down an unusual amount of earnest money for the local market or an earnest money deposit that equals the total down payment can raise red flags. Deposits made with several checks with inconsistent dates and check numbers, or information on a check (such as the name and address) that do not match that of the buyers, might also set them off. Excessive real estate commission, a contract dated after credit paperwork, or a contract that does not reflect a true negotiation are all indicators of trouble.

Mortgage applications may also contain red flags. Significant or conflicting modifications made from a handwritten to a typed application are another easily-detected red flag. It's also possible that the application isn't signed or dated. A post office box as the applicant's place of employment could potentially be a red flag. The buyer's personal and work phone numbers may be posted on the same page. Another red flag is a buyer who is currently residing in the subject property or who is purchasing an investment property and does not possess a primary residence. A loan application for a cash-out refinance on a recently acquired property or excessive payment shock, which could indicate a straw buyer or exaggerated income - are also red flags.

Discrepancies in social security numbers and addresses inside the loan file could be general red flags. Documentation that has been altered with deletions or correction fluid, numbers on the documentation that appear to be "squeezed" due to alteration, differences in handwriting or writing style within a document, or an excessive number of automated underwriting systems, are also red flags.

ADVERTISING

As you'll know, advertising is an obvious approach to allow the general public to understand more about what you do and how you can help them - and to make money off of that. In the mortgage market, advertisements are also common. There are, however, some regulations that must be obeyed. We'll go through many of the advertising do's and don'ts in the following section.

Advertisements According to Regulation Z

According to Regulation Z, an advertisement is considered:

- In any medium, a commercial message that supports a credit transaction, such as:
- Newspapers, flyers, brochures, and magazines (printed materials)
- Announcements on the radio, podcast, or television
- Electronic/digital advertisements on websites or social media
- Literature sent by direct mail
- Signs with printed elements on the inside or outside
- Calls or solicitations on the phone

*Reg Z does not perceive information provided to businesses as resources as advertisements.

MAP Ad Rule

Advertisements (according to the MAP Ad rule) are "any sort of oral statement, illustration, or portrayal that has the sole goal of effecting a sale or generating interest in the acquisition of a product or service."

The following are some examples of commercial communications:

1. Brochures, magazines, newspapers, booklets, or pamphlets are all examples of printed materials.

2. Radio, free television, or cable television are all options.
3. Internet
4. Letter
5. Posters, billboards, bench signs, and public transportation cards.
6. Script for telemarketing
7. Audio message over a telephone system
8. State Legislation

Advertisement definitions under state law are highly dependent on the state in question. Regulation Z, the MAP Ad regulation, and the SAFE Act all influence how advertisements are defined in different states. Ads cannot be used to deceive consumers or push products in a deceptive manner. They must also reveal certain details..

HELOC requirements, according to TILA Regulation Z, include:

- Trigger phrases that necessitate more disclosures
- Disclosures on variable rates, premium rates, balloon payments, and tax implications
- Detailed rate and payment disclosures
- Using deceptive terms, such as "free money," is prohibited.

1. Closed-ended mortgages have additional requirements..
2. Cannot display government endorsements in a false light
3. When advertising fixed rates and payments - rate of payment comparisons, claims of debt elimination, the lender's name, the use of foreign language, and the word "counselor" misleads the public.

Regulation N..

Regulation N details the restriction against misrepresentation of materials linked to mortgage lending arrangements. This includes the following:

- How much interest a consumer will pay each month, as well as whether/not unpaid interest will be applied to the total amount owed.
- Annual percentage rates (APRs), fees, charges, and prepayment penalties are all examples of annual percentage rates.
- Actual expenses of optional items, such as credit insurance.
- The minimum amount of insurance and taxes that a loan requires.

- When a variable rate mortgage is used instead of a fixed-rate mortgage, the term cannot be "fixed" used incorrectly.
- Comparing the rates and payments of a loan to the rates and payments that are only available for parts of a loan.
- The quantity of credit or cash available to you.
- The possibility of defaulting and the conditions surrounding it.
- The quantity, timing, and veracity of mandatory & minimum payments.
- The loan's ability to be used to consolidate or restructure debt.
- The channel via which customers communicate with you.
- Whether or not the loan, program, or supplier is linked to any government institutions or programs.
- When it comes to counseling, how much time do you have?
- The likelihood of a consumer obtaining a loan, refinance, or modification.

CFPB and FTC Regulations on Advertisements

The CFPB and the FTC are two agencies that regulate marketing and ensure that people and businesses follow the rules. Those in the mortgage sector do not want to be on the naughty list of these regulatory entities.

The CFPB keeps an eye out for the following things:

1. Misrepresentation of government allegiance
2. Implying that a certain rate available through a VA loan is part of some sort of stimulus scheme, and that the rate is about to expire.
3. Inaccurate information about interest rates. For instance, claiming a loan has a fixed rate when it actually has a variable rate.
4. Statements that are deceptive when it comes to reverse mortgages. For example, stating that there will be no payments but failing to mention that taxes and insurances must still be paid. Alternatively, saying that previous credit card debt will be eligible for a discount.
5. Possibly misrepresenting a customer's eligibility for a specific interest rate or term.

The FTC is on the lookout for the following items:

- Advertisements that promote incredibly low fixed rate mortgages while omitting to provide important loan details.
- Statements, visuals, abbreviations, or symbols that imply that an entity is connected to a government agency.

- Advertisements that guarantee approval and offer exceptionally low monthly payments while omitting to mention significant terms and limitations.

Violations of advertising regulations can have a variety of ramifications. Companies must have policies and procedures in place to ensure that all consumer advertisements and marketing materials are reviewed for legal compliance before being distributed. The importance of analyzing advertisements and marketing materials should be emphasized in employee training. In the end, we must constantly be cautious about what we publish in our adverts. We must be honest about our product offerings and their limitations. If we don't, there will be ethical and legal consequences.

ETHICAL PRACTICES IN THE LOAN ORIGINATION PROCESS

FINANCIAL RESPONSIBILITY

Loan originators, like borrowers, must demonstrate financial responsibility and ethics in their field of business. They must be capable of managing both their own and their clients' funds. Those seeking a license must be deemed suitable for licensing in the states in which they intend to do business. For example, previous bankruptcies or a history of bad credit management may make them unfit for licensing in many cases.

Loan originators must also demonstrate financial responsibility by collecting fees and payments in an ethical manner. Compensation for loan originators cannot be based on the terms of a transaction unless it is based on a percentage of the loan amount. They are also not permitted to obtain money from both the consumer AND a third party. Steering is a predatory lending practice in which a loan originator persuades a borrower to purchase a mortgage product only because it raises their loan compensation. The Loan Estimate must include the fees and compensation paid to the loan originator. Those fees have a zero-tolerance policy, which means they can't go up between the Loan Estimate and the Final Loan Estimate.

CLOSING DISCLOSURE

Fees paid to a lender, mortgage broker, or affiliate for a needed service cannot be increased as a result of changing circumstances. Application fees, origination fees, underwriting fees, processing fees, verification fees, and rate-lock fees are all common lender fees. Customers must be adequately informed by loan originators as accurately as possible, of what they're expected to pay at closure.

On a loan closing, they will need to account for their down payment along with closing fees minus any lender or seller credits. The consumer should not be slapped with any unexpected or excessive costs at closing, and they should never be left in a scenario where they are uncertain where their money has gone or is going. Customer funds must always be accounted for, and loan originators should be able to tell customers exactly where their money is going. RESPA prohibits referral fees and kickbacks, as we mentioned previously. Fees must be shared 50/50 and charged according to who performs the service, if fees are split across service providers.

HANDLING BORROWER COMPLAINTS

Even if they disagree with the complaint, loan originators must maintain a professional manner and respond to consumer complaints in the most efficient way feasible in order to address their issues. Consumers may simply be looking for reassurance during a difficult period, but their complaints must be handled seriously. Customers should be informed about how their concerns are being handled by loan originators.

- Problems With Consumers' Inability to Pay

The majority of the complaints received were from customers who were having trouble making payments. These individuals described lengthy loss mitigation processes in which their servicer repeatedly requested the same documentation. Consumers also complained about contradicting and misleading foreclosure warnings, which left them unsure of what would happen and when.

- Loan Transfers Can Be Perplexing

When their loans were transferred to another servicer, consumers frequently complained about misinformation or a lack of information. As a result, payments made during this period were not applied to their account since they were not sent to the correct location.

1. Problems Communicating with a Servicer

Consumers frequently complained about having trouble communicating with their loan service provider. Their main issues were that the information provided by the servicer was confusing, and their problems were not addressed. Because of the communication challenges, they had to wait longer to get the resolutions they needed on their mortgage loans.

According to the Consumer Financial Protection Bureau, the top complained-about corporations were Bank of America, Wells Fargo, Ocwen, and Nationstar Mortgage.

MORTGAGE COMPANY

Compliance self-reporting violations by mortgage companies are frequently held accountable. They must report any violations to the appropriate regulatory authorities, explain how the matter was resolved, and how it will be handled in the future to prevent it from happening again. Mortgage businesses may be able to reduce their fines by self-reporting (reporting before infractions are discovered through a regulatory examination).

Loan originators have the power to contact a consumer on behalf of a lender to market the lender's goods, prices, and terms. These products must be tailored to the demands of the customer, while also taking into account their financial history. The loan originator can start the application process, provide credit conditions, negotiate terms, and even extend credit to the customer. If a loan originator learns new information about a consumer that is not reported on their credit report, the loan originator must alert the lender about that fact, as it may impair the client's ability to qualify for a loan product. It is illegal and unethical to withhold this type of information. Employer information must also be verified by loan originators. The borrower's most recent pay stubs, W-2s, or a Verification of Employment which confirms that the borrower is employed and has a stable income, can all be used to verify employment. The borrower must give a two-year history of overtime or fluctuating income for qualification reasons, and the borrower's employer must certify that the income is projected to continue. Loan originators must be licensed if they accept loan applications, negotiate loan terms, or seek compensation for a loan. Three hours of federal law and regulation, three hours of ethical training, and two hours of training on lending requirements for atypical mortgage products must be included in pre-licensing coursework. Some states may have specific additional requirements. In order to verify that all state-specific requirements have been met, applicants must fill out and submit form MU4.

RELATIONSHIPS WITH CONSUMERS

Loan originators have a fiduciary responsibility with their consumers & customers, which means they must prioritize their customers' financial well-being over their own. Under the Gramm-Leach-Bliley Act and the Safeguards provisions, borrower information must be kept private. To protect borrower information and limit access to unauthorized individuals, loan originators must take the necessary precautions. A mortgage typically requires a down payment of three to twenty percent. Borrowing more money to meet down payment fees is not permitted by lenders because it will affect the borrower's debt-to-income ratio, amongst other requirements.

If there is no evidence that the money must be repaid, it is possible to use gifted funds for a down payment. It's also possible that you'll be able to use gifted funds for the complete down payment. Lenders may demand the present-giver to sign a gift letter that includes their contact information, the gift amount, and a statement that the gift is not requiring repayment. While some loan programs may allow a borrower to qualify for grants or financial help, many lenders prefer down payment sources that come directly from the applicant, as this signals a lower risk for the lender.

Mortgage Loan originators may charge discount points, which are used to lower a mortgagee's interest rate. The charge is paid in advance as a percentage of the loan amount by the borrower. These programs are not available from all lenders, and the rates may vary. One percent of the loan amount is equal to one discount point. In certain cases, a proxy can be used. The loan originator has to know how broad the power of attorney is. A restricted or general power of attorney can be used. A limited power of attorney can only manage the tasks specified in the document, whereas a general power of attorney can handle all financial problems. Because the use of a power of attorney may imply fraud, the underwriter must approve it.

Prior to a loan estimate, and before the borrower declares an intent to proceed, loan originators may seek credit reports. A tri-merge (which is a merged credit report created from information obtained from all three major credit reporting agencies) may be requested by the loan originator. The qualifying score is the lowest of three scores for two or more borrowers, or the middle of three scores for one borrower. The credit score requirements for each loan product may differ. The loan originator must get explicit consent from the applicant in order to pull their credit report. The Borrower Authorization Form is a document signed by an applicant that authorizes the lender to verify and receive information and documentation from third parties as needed in connection with a mortgage loan application.

The loan originator must notify the lender if any modifications are made to the borrower's loan file at any time. The individuals that must sign the mortgage are the ones who will be liable for repaying the debt. Borrowers, co-borrowers, and co-signers are all included. An individual's salary cannot be utilized for qualification, if they are not going to be on the loan. If a loan originator is also a real estate agent or has a family member who owns less than one percent of a third-party company, they must provide an Affiliated Business Disclosure form to the borrower. At the time of a referral, a conflict of interest disclosure must also be supplied.

Appraisals cannot be ordered directly by loan originators; instead, they must be ordered through an Appraisal Management Company, which is then responsible for assigning the appraisal to an appraiser. Any questions about the appraisal must be sent to the Appraisal Management Company, including any inaccuracies on the report or any extra information required.

According to the Equal Credit Opportunity Act, applicants must receive a copy of the appraisal report within three business days of the loan closing. Undisclosed income on a loan application will distort the debt-to-income ratios that are vital in calculating how much a borrower can afford. Undisclosed income could include revenue from a second employment, part-time job, or seasonal job, as well as rental or room-share income. Public assistance income can be used for qualification criteria if the loan product allows it. The income and asset amounts utilized to qualify for the loan must match the bank statements and income verifications. Debts and obligations taken on after a loan closes are a further source of unknown information that could skew these ratios.

Applicants should also disclose to a lender if they are applying for loans from other lenders, so that they are not flagged for fraudulent schemes. Digital files must be safeguarded in the same way that conventional files are. Password-protected computers, tablets, and phones, as well as other devices, are recommended. For at least five years following, files must be kept confidential and safe.

TRUTH IN MARKETING AND ADVERTISING

Misrepresentations in ads for mortgage services are prohibited under Regulation N. Deceptive claims in mortgage advertisements provided to customers by mortgage brokers, lenders, and advertising firms are prohibited by the rule. In order for a product's dangers and benefits to be properly defined, it must be advertised.

All pertinent information (such as the interest rate, APR, loan product, and program details) should be presented so that the borrower can make an informed decision. The advertisement may also include property information such as availability, features, amenities, and pricing. Advertisements should include information that is relevant to the broadest possible audience. It should, however, be balanced by not overdoing it.

In their advertising, most lenders use the Equal Housing Opportunity logo or its accompanying text. To ensure compliance, loan originators should consult local and state rules as well as their company's policies.

BORROWER EDUCATION

Borrowers must be presented with clear options, and loan originators must educate them so that they completely understand each product they are being offered. If a loan originator believes a borrower may not completely comprehend a mortgage product, the loan originator can recommend that the borrower schedule a counseling meeting with one of the HUD-approved homeowner counseling agencies or a financial advisor.

GENERAL BUSINESS ETHICS

If a loan officer suspects that the information provided by an applicant is false, they have the authority to reject the application. Loan originators, on the other hand, should normally not reject an application until they notice any red flags. If mortgage fraud is discovered during the loan process, the originating lender may initiate a buyback, the note may be called due, and any premium fees may be returned. If loan originators suspect an applicant is supplying incorrect information, they must submit suspicious files to the Compliance Officer. In order to create eligibility for a borrower, loan originators should not change or falsify any documentation. If they are not accurate about the borrower's capacity to qualify for a given loan program, they may be fined or fired.

When a borrower asks for help with a loan product, the loan originator should avoid telling the borrower what to do. Their main focus should be on educating the borrower about the loan product and evaluating their financial history to determine what would be most beneficial to them. The borrower should have the ultimate decision on when to lock in an interest rate. Unsolicited counsel should never be given by the loan originator. Furthermore, conversations and instruction should revolve around the loan products of which the borrower exhibits interest.

When an outside party requests information regarding a loan or borrower, the loan originator should refer the party to the customer directly. The client should be able to choose whether or not their information is shared, especially if sharing the information isn't required to qualify for a loan product.

The moral rules that govern how a corporation serves its customers and treats its staff are known as business ethics. While certain conduct may be considered illegal, others are unacceptable. We'll go through some of the key elements of business ethics that you should adhere to here:

Transparency

This entails accurately representing the facts, always delivering the complete and utter truth, and clearly conveying what is going on in the business. Transparency is the cornerstone of a healthy customer connection, which in turn leads to increased corporate and business success. The more open and honest a company is, the greater public trust it will receive. Transparency is especially important during public relations crises when people are on edge. Businesses make mistakes, but it's worse when they try to hide them.

Integrity

Regardless of public pressure, if you believe in a decision you're going to make, stick to it. This exemplifies honor and bravery. Companies with noteworthy character do what they believe is right, even if others disagree. This will help to maintain public trust.

Trustworthiness

Businesses gain trustworthiness when they keep their promises to the people they work with. They follow through on what they say they'll do and when they say they'll do it. Customers are concerned not only with the quality of your products and services, but also with the level of trust they may place in you. Keeping promises demonstrates that you are dependable and principled.

Loyalty

Loyalty refers to a company's interactions with its employees, partners, investors, contractors, and customers. When there is loyalty, firms will make decisions that benefit all of the connections involved. Loyalty demonstrates that organizations place a higher priority on growth and their employees than on their own personal demands.

Fairness

When competing in the free market, businesses should operate fairly and avoid cheating and other unethical tactics in order to obtain an advantage. Equality and treating people equally are other good examples of fairness. This might be related to employment methods, business collaborations, marketing campaigns, and customer acquisition tactics.

If a firm, for example, lies about its competitors in order to steal clients, that is unethical. This can also include refusing to hire someone because of their color, gender, or religion, among other factors.

Compassion

Companies that practice ethics are genuine in their kindness, compassion, and concern. This means that in business, they are attempting to produce goodness through their methods. When making a decision, it's important to think about how it may affect others, including people outside the firm. The goal is to limit unfavorable effects while increasing positive ones.

Respect

Is the basic regard for people's rights, privacy, and dignity, both inside and beyond the organization. Businesses that treat all people equally, regardless of ethnicity or religion, are viewed positively in the public eye. For both moral and legal reasons, businesses are obligated to keep certain information private. Maintaining a level of privacy further demonstrates that a business adheres to a set of industry-specific laws.

Lawfulness

Following corporate ethics principles also includes complying with applicable laws and regulations. Tax evasion, harassment, discrimination, and workplace safety violations, for example, all come with a slew of legal ramifications. Companies that operate within the bounds of the law have a higher level of credibility, which contributes to an improved public image.

Providing Outstanding Service

Companies must always try to serve clients and customers with the highest quality products and services. They are always looking for better ways to deliver their goods and are striving to improve their performance. Businesses that are striving for success are never satisfied and are continuously seeking ways to improve.

Responsibility

Companies must be aware of their obligations to clients and staff. Because they will set the tone, their leadership will have an impact on how the company operates. Businesses have a responsibility to lead value-based decisions that benefit all stakeholders. What a leader accomplishes will be emulated by his or her followers. As a result, organizational leaders should set an example of the ethical standards they expect others to follow.

Maintaining a Positive Public Image

An ethical business strives to keep its public image intact. This entails acting in a way that benefits the company. If a company's reputation is harmed by an activity taken within it, the firm must respond immediately and effectively in a way that benefits everyone. Through the reconciliation process, businesses must demonstrate openness, accountability, and responsibility.

Overall, good business ethics ensures that businesses are operating legally, creating customer trust, and pleasing clients and shareholders, while recruiting and managing a diverse group of high-performing employees.

CHAPTER SEVEN

HOW TO OVERCOME TEST ANXIETY

Test anxiety is more than apprehension before a test; it can also be an acute fear or worry. This is because test anxiety is a form of performance anxiety, which is when you are under pressure to perform well in a given setting. Performance anxiety may relate to sexual performance, examination performance, relationship performance, or sports performance, just to name a few. Generally, this anxiety stems from unresolved fears regarding something that happened in the past, which you perceived to be a negative experience. So, the anxiety is that you fear it will happen again, and you fear the negative emotions it may bring inside of you, or how said experience may make others perceive you. Anxiety of any kind, including test anxiety, can have both a physical and mental impact. Exam anxiety can make it difficult for you to perform well on a test, unless you have a strategy to handle it. Fortunately, you'll learn the best strategies in this chapter.

COMMON CAUSES OF ANXIETY

The Fear of Failure - Taking a significant test can put you under a lot of stress. You're under pressure to do well on the test, which can be motivating, but you're also concerned that failing the test would reflect poorly on your character, or that a dismal grade will reveal your true worth.

Inadequate Planning - You may believe that you are well prepared and will perform well on the exam, so you will put off studying until the last minute. You could also decide not to study at all. In either case, test anxiety may arise on the day of the exam.

High Pressure - Knowing you need to receive a certain grade to pass a class or perhaps get a job might put you under a lot of pressure, which can lead to test anxiety.

Poor Test History - Failure to perform well on a previous test may cause you to become worried when taking the next one. It's preferable if you concentrate on the test at hand rather than thinking about how you performed on previous assessments.

Biological Causes of Test Anxiety - When you're in a stressful scenario, your body produces an adrenaline-like hormone. The "fight-or-flight" reaction is triggered by this hormone, which prepares your body to deal with stressful events. This response aids you in deciding whether to stay and deal with the stress at hand or to leave the situation. You can have trouble focusing on the test if your fight-or-flight reflex initiates. Sweating, trembling hands, and nausea are all possible side effects.

Mental Causes of Test Anxiety - There are both biological and psychological causes of test anxiety. High expectations are one factor. For example, if a student believes they will perform poorly on a test, they would most likely experience anxiety both before and during the test. Another mental reason for test anxiety is having had test anxiety in the past. After experiencing test anxiety, you may develop a phobia of experiencing it again the next time you take a significant test.

REASONS WHY INDIVIDUALS FAIL TESTS

1. Inadequate Planning

The most common reason why students fail the NMLS exam is because of a lack of planning. Many students feel that taking the 20-hour Pre-Licensing course is sufficient preparation for passing the NMLS exam; however, this is not the case..

The Pre-Licensing Course is designed to give you the information you need to enter "into" the mortgage market — which isn't always what you'll need to pass the exam. To be well prepared for the exam, we recommend you study for an EXTRA 15 to 20 hours.

Again, the Pre-Licensing Course is designed to teach you about the mortgage industry as a whole, not to prepare you for an exam.

It covers the rules, regulations, and ideas that the NMLS wants you to understand, but not all of the knowledge is exam-based, and many test-takers rely only on the 20-hour pre-licensing class to pass the exam, which is simply insufficient.

2. Taking the Wrong Pre-Licensing Class

You enrolled in the incorrect Pre-Licensing course!!! Typically, students choose for the least expensive version – or an online only education.

An online self-study course may NOT be the greatest solution for you if you're new to the industry (or even if you aren't) because these classes essentially require you to "teach yourself." The issue here is that most Online Courses are learner-led and self-paced, which means you don't know who to turn to for help when you have issues, queries, or simply lose interest and fall behind in your studies. Instead, we recommend taking a "LIVE" course where you and the instructor are both in the same classroom whenever possible.

3. Not Having a Studying Strategy

"If you fail to plan, you plan to fail."

This one doesn't really need much explaining. Create a plan, choose the hours you'll study each day or week, and use all the resources available to you to fully grasp the content & be able to pass the practice exams with ease. Then, you'll be ready, and confident.

4. Don't wait too long

Many students fail the test as a result of an erratic study regimen or waiting too long to take it.

Here's what you should know: rules and regulations change frequently, and the exam does as well, so the longer you delay to take the exam, it's more likely the content will become outdated. Furthermore, the longer you wait, the more the knowledge you've learned will fade, and you will forget it. It has already changed seven times, and it will change again with a new administration. The longer you delay, the more the information will change, and the more likely you will fail the exam!

5. No Clue About the Test Outline?

Most students don't know the latest NMLS test outline. The NMLS provided a revised Test-Content Outline about what will be on the exam early last year. Just search 'NMLS Test Outline" to find it online. It would be like running across the state without a map if you study at random, without comprehending the NMLS Outline for what exactly will be on the exam.

You must also be aware of the five (5) categories and their respective weightings:

- Mortgage Loan Origination activities (25%)
- General Mortgage Knowledge (23%)
- Federal Mortgage-Related Laws (23%)
- Ethics (16%)
- Uniform State Examination (13%)

14 More Tips to Help Test Anxiety

1. Start preparing early - It is crucial that you begin studying for the test as soon as possible as opposed to cramming facts at the last minute. Begin revising a few weeks before the exam, and break it up into smaller chunks each day.

2. Make a study schedule - It is important to have a study strategy in place in order to succeed on an exam. A study plan will help you to set out time each day to study as well as mark out exactly what you'll be studying. Make a study schedule from the day you begin studying and stick to it all the way until the day of the test.

3. Learn how to study - Even if you think you've got it down, you can always learn more about how to study properly.

4. Maintain a positive attitude - Keep in mind that the outcome of a test has no bearing on your self-worth. Maintain a positive mindset and remind yourself that you can and will pass the test. Having faith in oneself and maintaining a positive attitude while studying and taking the test can go a long way!

5. Take your time when reading - Whether you have test anxiety or not, this is critical for any test. Before you begin the test, read the instructions carefully and read each question properly before selecting an answer. If you don't read everything thoroughly, you may miss a vital element.

6. Practice tests should be your best friend - Practice tests are an excellent approach to ensure that you are fully prepared for your exam. You'll be able to receive a personal peek at the exam, including how many questions there will be and the types of questions you may expect. You'll also have a better sense of the areas you need to improve.

7. Have a restful night's sleep - Make sure you get a decent night's sleep the night before the exam; at least 8 hours is advised. A good night's sleep can help you improve your memory and concentration and make you feel refreshed and ready to take that test the next day.

8. Begin with what you already know - You do not have to begin with the first question when taking the test. Begin with those you are familiar with. Don't

waste time attempting to answer that one question that has stumped you. Skip it and go on to the next one you're familiar with. Return to the questions you skipped and try to answer them at the end if time allows.

9. Arrive at the test place early on the day of the test - Rushing because you're late is something you don't want to do here. Rushing to get to the exam because you're late will just increase your worry on the day of the exam. Arrive a little early at the test place. Walk around the building or do some stretches to help you relax if you're feeling anxious. Moving your body will help you feel better by removing some of that nervous energy and getting your blood flowing.

10. Remember to eat and drink - To function and work effectively, your brain and body require sustenance. Make sure you eat a small healthy meal and drink enough water on the day. Sugary drinks and caffeinated beverages, such as coffee, should be avoided. Caffeinated beverages might make you jittery and increase your anxiety levels. But you know yourself best.

11. Maintain your concentration - On test day, try to concentrate solely on the test. Don't be concerned with what you'll do after the exam or what happened before it, and don't worry about how the other test takers are doing. Concentrate entirely on the exam at hand.

12. Wear comfortable clothing - Dress professionally, but in something that makes you feel at ease and allows you to unwind. Avoid clothing that you will have to adjust frequently, or that is too tight for you. In case the test room is too cool for you, bring a light jacket or sweater.

13. If necessary, rest - Take a little pause if you feel your test anxiety is getting the better of you. Close your eyes, take 10 deep breaths in and 10 deep breaths out, then turn your attention back to the exam.

14. Keep distractions to a minimum - Don't be concerned about the person in front of you or next to you who may be completing their test twice as quickly as you. Concentrate on your test by sitting somewhere free of distractions, preferably towards the front of the room.

YOUR STUDY STRATEGY

If you want to understand some more effective strategies for studying and being educated on a subject, keep reading. It's time to unearth a few of these mysteries.

#1 The 3Rs.

Reading, reciting, and reviewing are the three Rs. If you've been given the task of reading a chapter, the first step is to read it. But don't read the entire chapter at once; instead, read a portion of it before closing the book and putting any notes away. The next stage is to recall everything you can about what you just read and recite it. You can recite it in front of a mirror, your favorite pet, a study partner, or just when sitting in your room. After you've finished reciting, review the section again to see how much you recall and where you went wrong. This strategy may appear to be time-consuming, but it actually saves time because you are actively trying to learn rather than merely going through the motions. The following step is one of the reasons why this strategy is effective.

#2 Go Deep

When you read a book for the purpose of learning something new, you can't just skim through it like you would a social media page. You won't remember anything if you do it this way. Your mind is not a sponge that absorbs everything it comes into contact with. You must analyze the data until it remains in place. This will tell your brain that the material you're reviewing is important enough to remember. Connecting new information to what you already know is a terrific method to remember and keep it.

#3 Let your imagination run wild.

Concepts that can be visualized are more likely to be remembered by students. Making images in your mind interact with one another is an important part of this approach. These visuals don't need to be strange; they just need to be memorable and interactive.

#4 Keep Your Head Up and Your Pen Down

You must pay whole attention throughout a lecture, or you will miss key details. Keep your attention on the lecture and avoid talking to your neighbor, looking around the room, texting, or doing anything else that isn't relevant to it. This is the moment to pay attention and take detailed notes. You must strike a balance between the accuracy of the notes and the avoidance of turning them into a manuscript. Consider how the lecture relates to something you already know when you listen to an instructor in class. Instead of lengthy sentences or paragraphs, write down a few crucial words and phrases. This will make the information more meaningful and will help you avoid reading filler words until you find anything useful. Even if you can record a lecture or if the instructor posts slides on their website, you will simply be reading them without making any actual impression. Because slides and recordings cannot think for you, you should still take appropriate notes during a lecture.

Finally, Don't Forget What You've Learned. Students have a tendency to pass over facts that they believe they already know. This is not a strategy we recommend. Instead, retest yourself on these principles to make sure you understand them.

With all of that, you should be confident in passing your exam with flying colors. What follows next is more than 200 practice questions and answers that you can use at any time in order to prepare for your NMLS exam. We've included both written questions as well as mathematical questions. All that's left to say now, is good luck! We wish you all of the luck in the world in your future career as a Mortgage Loan Originator, as well as much prosperity!

Yours, KNG Education

CHAPTER EIGHT
PRACTICE TEST 1

1.)RESPA aids in the regulation of which of the following?

A.) The use of technology and digital security in mortgage origination

B.) Kickbacks

C.) Advertising trigger phrases

D.) All of the above

2.) Within how many working days of receipt a loan application should the Good Faith Estimate or Loan Estimate be given to a borrower??

A.) 3 working days

B.) 5 working days

C.) 10 working days

D.) 30 working days

3.) Red Flags Rule extends instructions for?

A.) Disclosures about the loan

B.) Qualification for a loan

C.) Kickbacks

D.) Theft of identity

4.) A mortgage is considered high cost under the Home Ownership and Equity Protection Act (HOEPA) if the total points and fees exceed what % of the loan amount?

A.) 5%

B.) 8%

C.) 10%

D.) 15%

5.) On which timeframe should the borrower receive the Affiliated Business Arrangement disclosure?

A.) Within three working days of submitting an application for a loan

B.) At closing

C.) At loan consummation

D.) At the time of the referral or shortly thereafter

6.) After conducting an analysis of escrow accounts, how much must an escrow account be overpaid by to allow the borrower to get a refund?

A.) $50

A.) $75

C.) $100

D.) Any money owed to the borrower must be returned.

7.) Once a borrower's loan has been fully paid off, what will they be issued?

A.) The repayment of a loan

B.) A mortgage discharge

C.) A form for canceling a note

D.) A fully paid-up mortgage note

8.) What does the ECOA entitle consumers to receive a copy of?

A.) The appraisal report on the property

B.) A copy of their credit report

C.) Statements of their mortgages

D.) All of the above

9.) Which of the following things may lenders use to determine loan eligibility?

A.) Your age

B.) Relationship status

C.) Sexuality

D.) Ability to pay back

10.)Which of these describes an affiliated business relationship that must be disclosed?

A.)Two businesses that refer business to each other on a regular basis in exchange for a predetermined fee for each transaction.

B.)A large corporation with several offices that refers business to one another.

C.)A lender that owns a stake in a settlement company that is utilized to settle claims arranging the closing on one of their transactions for a charge

D.)A broker who purchases leads from a company in order to gain the contact information of a possible client.

11.) Which of these transactions doesn't allow the borrower a Right to Rescind?

A.) A refinance loan

B.) A purchase loan

C.) A cash-out refinance

D.) A loan for home improvements

12.)After receiving a loan application, how many working days should the statement of Mortgage Servicing Disclosure be delivered to the borrower?

A.) 1 working day

B.) 2 working days

C.) 3 working days

D.) 4 working days

13.) Which one of the following is authorized by the Home Mortgage Disclosure Act (HMDA)?

A.) It requires the disclosure of the loan amount.

B.) It demands the reporting of the property's location.

C.) It demands the disclosure of the borrower's race.

D.) All of the above

14.) Which law stipulates financial institutions to post privacy advisories and to protect customers' personal information?

A.) Real Estate Settlement Procedures Act (RESPA)

B.) The Truth-in-Lending Act (TILA)

C.) The Gramm-Leach-Bliley Act (GLBA)

15.) Among the following, which one is a function of the FACTA?

A.) It entitles customers to a free credit report once a year.

B.) It makes unlawful kickbacks illegal.

C.) It establishes protected classes against which lenders are prohibited from discriminating.

D.) None of the preceding

. . .

16.) How many billing cycles must the Special Information Booklet be delivered to a borrower following obtaining a loan request?

A.) 1 working day

B.) 3 working days

C.) 7 working days

D.) 10 working days

17.) What should a loan originator do if a loan applicant refuses to reveal their ethnicity?

A.) Require the loan applicant to reveal their nationality.

B.) Refuse to take the application into consideration.

C.) Make an educated guess based on what you see.

D.) None of the preceding

18.) How many days after getting a Loan Estimate must an applicant indicate purpose to Continue?

A.) Five days

B.) 10 days

C.) 15 days

D.) 20 days

. . .

19.) How many hours of pre-licensing instruction is required for a loan originator to become licensed?

A.) 5 hours

B.) 10 hours

C.) 15 hours

D.) 20 hours

20.) How frequently must MLOs renew their licenses?

A.) Every year

B.) Every 2 years

C.) Every 5 years

D.) Every 10 years

21.) Within how many days of receiving a complete application, lenders should notify clients of any adverse action taken?

- 21 days
- 30 days
- 45 days
- 60 days

22.) To what law does Regulation V apply?

A.) The Truth in Lending Act

B.)The Home Ownership and Equity Protection Act

C.)The Real Estate Settlement Procedures Act

D.)The Fair Credit Reporting Act

23.) Which of the following is the mortgagor?

A.) The creditor

B.) The borrower

C.) Freddie Mac

D.) Fannie Mae

24.) What are the different types of liens that come with getting a mortgage?

A.) A voluntary lien

B.) An unintentional lien

C.) A mechanic's lien

D.) A tax lien

25.) What date determines an alien's position?

A.) The signing date

B.) The recording date

C.) The date upon which loan was approved

D.) The date on which the title search was conducted.

26.) When the customer receives revised disclosures before closing on a fixed-rate loan, how much variance in the APR is required?

A.)one-eighth of a percent

B.) a quarter of a percent

C.) One-fifth of a percent

D.) a third of a percentage point

27.) After the first mortgage lien, what phrase is used to represent liens that are recorded?

A.) Liens of estoppel

B.) Liens of mechanics

C.) Junior liens

D.) None of the above

28.) Which of the following statements concerning FHA loans is correct?

A.) FHA loans are backed by insurance.

B.) FHA loans are not transferable.

C.) There is a 5% late fee on FHA loans.

D.) All of the above

29.) To compute the fully indexed rate on an adjustable-rate mortgage once it starts to adjust, which of the following two must be added together?

A.) The cap and the margin

B.) The index and the margin

C.) The current index as well as the current interest rate

D.) None of the above

30.) What is the maximum interest rate for the second adjustment period of a 15-year ARM with a beginning interest rate of 3.75 percent, an adjustment rate cap of 2.25 percent, and a lifetime ceiling of 9 percent?

A.) 4%

B.) 7.25%

C.) 9%

D.) 8.25%

. . .

31.) What is the name for the act of transferring ownership, right, title, or interests in a property from one entity to another?

A.) Deed of Quit Claim

B.) Conveyance

C.) Transfer of Servicing

D.) Subordination

32.) When does the rescission period for an owner-occupied refinance deal subject to the Regulation Z right of recession expire if the transaction closes on a Monday, assuming no federal holidays throughout the week?

A.) Tuesday

B.) Wednesday

C.) Thursday

D.) Friday

33.) Which of the following mortgages would need a borrower need private mortgage insurance (PMI) for?

A.) A traditional loan with a 16 percent down payment

B.) An FHA loan requiring a down payment of less than 21%

C.) A 25 percent down payment on a Jumbo loan

D.) An 8 percent down payment on a VA loan

34.) What is the meaning of PITI?

A.) Property, interest, title, and index

B.) Prepayment, index, term, and interest

C.) Pay down, insurance, trust, and interest

D.) Principal, interest, taxes, and insurance

35.) In a gift letter, which of the following must be included?

A.) The name/address of the gifter

B.) The $ value of the present

C.) A statement stating that the gift is not refundable.

D.) All of the above

36.) For a $350,000 loan, how much does a 2 and a half discount point cost?

A.) $2,500

B.) $7.750

C.) $8,750

D.) $10.875

37.) How much interest would the borrower owe for the days remaining in the month if a $300,000 loan with a 7% interest rate is closed on a property with a purchase price of $340,000 and there are 8 days left in the month?

A.) $389.75

B.) $426.53

C.) $460.27

D.) $512.35

38.) For a home with a purchase price of $250,000, an appraisal of $240,000, and an LTV ratio of 80%, what is the loan amount?

- $190,000
- $192.000
- $195,000
- $200,000

39.) With a $1920 PITI payment, a $240 condo fee, and a gross monthly income of $9,600, what would the housing expense ratio be?

A.) 18.75 percent

B.) 16.50 percent

C.) 17.25 percent

D.) 22.50 percent

40.) What is a homeowner's total monthly income if they work 50 hours a week and earn $15 per hour?

A.) $2, 740

B.) $2,703

C.) $3,250

D.) $2,900

41.) What is the late charge fee for a borrower with a VA (veterans affairs) loan of $400,000, monthly P&I of $1,600, annual PMI of $1,850, annual hazard insurance of $2,500, and annual property taxes of $ 3,800?

A.) $58

B.) $64

C.)$60

D.) $100

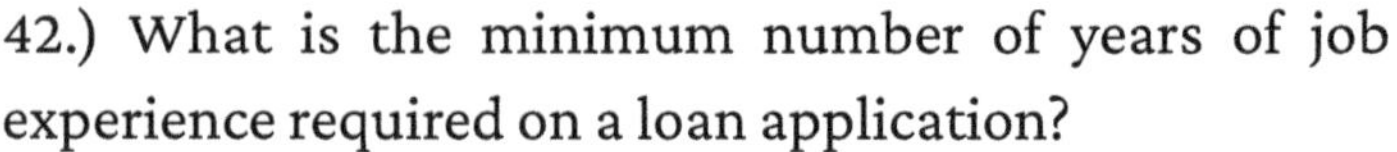

42.) What is the minimum number of years of job experience required on a loan application?

A.) 2 years

B.) 3 years

C.) 4 years

D.) 5 years

43.) When calculating monthly debt based on information from a credit report, what proportion of the total is used if no minimum monthly credit card payment is stated?

A.) 5%

B.) 7%

C.) 8%

D.) 3%

44.) Do bankruptcies stay on a person's credit report for a long time?

A.) 5 years

B.) 7 years

C.) 10 years

D.) 12 years

45.) For a single-borrower loan, what is the indicative credit rating if the lender obtains two credit-worthiness?

A.) The higher of the two scores

B.) The lower of the two scores

C.) The average of the two scores

D.) It depends on the lender's policies

46.) If the closing date is August 21, when is the first mortgage payment due?

A.) October 1st

B.) July Ist

C.) September 1st

D.) August Ist

47.) Who is qualified to receive a real estate broker's referral fee?

A.) Past customers

B.) Other real estate broker firms

C.) Closing agents

D.) All of the above

48.) What is the most prevalent type of mortgage fraud?

A.) Deflated appraisals

B.) Encroachments

C.) Both A & B

D.) Equity skimming

49.) What is the acronym for APR?

A.) Annual Price of Refinancing

B.) Average Prime Offer Rate

C.) Annual Percentage of Rates

D.) Average Percentage of Rates

50.) A loan given to a low-credit creditor is referred to by which of the following terms?

A.) Subordinate

B.) Jumbo

C.) Subprime

D.) None of the above

51.) What kind of financial crime involves a group of culprits applying for a mortgage with a fictitious borrower and assets?

A.) Air loans

B.) Double selling

C.) Short sale fraud

D.) Chunking

52.)What loan-to-value ratio permits the lender's obligation for private mortgage insurance (PMII) to be canceled?

A.) 40 percent

B.) 60 percent

C.) 78 percent

D.) 80 percent

53.) Which of the relevant documentation may a salaried employee be required to provide in order to obtain a loan?

A.) The previous 90 day's pay stubs

B.) A profit and loss statement

C.) The previous 2 year's W-2s

D.) All of the above

54.)What forms of loans are available for rural properties?

A.) VA loans

B.) USDA loans

C.) FHA loans

D.) ARM loans

55.) Which term describes a property's increase in value?

A.) Appreciation

B.) Acceleration

C.) Prepayment

D.) Depreciation

56.)How long are credit reports valid once they've been pulled for qualification purposes?

A.) 30 days

B.) 60 days

C.) 90 days

D.) 120 days

57.) The FBI identifies two types of mortgage fraud. What are they?

A.) Domestic mortgage fraud and international mortgage fraud

B.) Appraisal fraud and application fraud

C.) Criminal mortgage fraud and misdemeanor mortgage fraud

D.) Fraud for profit and fraud for housing

58.) A purchaser will not buy more for one asset than for another of equivalent value, according to which of the following hypothesese?

A.) The Highest and Best Use Principle

B.) The Substitution Principle

C.) The Market Value Principle

D.) The Conformity Principle

. . .

59.) In what type of mortgage fraud is a borrower who has no intention of repaying the loan?

A.) Fictitious loans

B.) Air loans

C.) Mortgage servicing fraud

D.) Property flipping

60.) What of the following is a sign of mortgage fraud?

A.) Changes between a handwritten and typed application

B.) A borrower who is purchasing an investment property but does not possess a primary home.

C.) Verifications completed over the weekend or on a holiday

D.) All of the above

61.) Which of the following forms is used to verify information about a job? A.) Verification of Deposit

B.) Verification of Employment

C.) The Loan Application

D.) None of the above

• • •

62.) What is the alternative name for Fannie Mae's automated underwriting system?

A.) Desktop Underwriter

B.) Loan Prospector

C.) Fannie Mae Underwriting

D.) None of the above

63.) Which of the following words describes the most likely price at which an asset will be sold on the open market?

A.) Estimated value

B.) Appraisal value

C.) Market value

D.) None of the above

64.) What is the most often utilized residential appraisal method?

A.) Market Approach

B.) Cost Approach

C.) Income Approach

D.) All of the above

. . .

65.) Using the Income Method, what is a property's value with a $50,000 annual net operating income and a 9% capitalization rate?

A.) $555,555.56

B.)$480,869.38

C.) $310.000

D.)$222,584.95

66.)Which organization handles mortgage refusal complaints?

A.) HUD

B.) FCC

C.) CFPB

D.) All of the above

67.)Which of the following permits someone other than the owner of the property to be on the property for a particular reason?

A.) An easement

B.) An encumbrance

C.) An encroachment

D.) A title

. . .

68.) Which one of the following guidelines refers to a property's most profitable and acceptable use?

A.) The Principle of Substitution

B.) The Principle of Competition

C.) The Principle of Change

D.) The Principle of Highest & Best Use

69.) What term is used to describe a claim on a property that may limit its ability to be sold?

A.) An easement

B.) A quitclaim deed

C.) An assumable mortgage

D.) A title defect

70.) What is the phrase for when a lender sells a mortgage to another lender?

A.) Note transfer

B.) Assignment of mortgage

C.) Servicing transfer

D.) Warehouse lending

. . .

71.) If a loan broker wants the customer's consent to obtain copies of their tax returns of their income, the prospective customer must sign what form?

A.) Form 4506-T

B.) Verification of Tax Filing

C.) Verification of Income

D.) None of the above

72.) Which lien is paid firstly during a foreclosure sale?
A.) The lien recorded first

B.) The lien in the subordinate position

C.) The property tax lien

D.) The lien with the largest balance

73.) If a lender refuses to give security-backed loans in a certain neighborhood due to the ethnic or racial design of the area, they are committing the prohibited act of?

A.)Steering

B.) Redlining

C.) Coercion

D.) Reconveyance

74.) If a mortgage advertisement implies a rate of finance charge, how must it state the rate?

A.)The interest rate

B.)The APR

C.)The rate without any points

D.) None of the above

75.) Of the following choices, which expense associated with a home loan is NOT paid from an escrow account?

A.) Title fees

B.) Property taxes

C.) Homeowners insurance

D.) Flood insurance

76.) According to the Equal Credit Opportunity Act, which of the following sources of income may be eliminated for the purpose of qualifying the borrower's income??

A.) Child support

B.) Alimony

C.) Short term disability

D.) Social Security Income

77.) The interest rate estimate provided on a Loan Estimate must be available for at least how many working days after the applicant is awarded the loan.

A.) 3

B.) 5

C.)7

D.) None of the above

78.)What type of mortgage fraud has an applicant committed if he/she purposefully withholds information that would preclude him from acquiring a mortgage loan?

A.) Ignorance

B.) Terrorism

C.) Falsification

D.) Collusion

. . .

79.) If a borrower makes $4300 in gross monthly income, what is the maximum "total" debt allowed for them by a conventional lender?

A.) $1500

B.) $1,720

C.) $1.570

D.) $1,482

80.) Which of the following fees would NOT be considered a finance charge in the APR calculation?

A.) Mortgage protection insurance

B.) Points of discount

C.) Fees associated with the start-up of a business

D.) Hazard insurance escrow deposit

81). If a homeowner "buys down" the interest rate on their loan, how would that reflect on the Loan Estimate?

A.) A creditor's charge

B.) A lender's yield spread premium

C.) A loan to a borrower

D.) A fee levied against the borrower

. . .

82.) What is the age requirement for a reverse mortgage borrower?

A.) 59

B.) 60

C.) 62

D.) 65

83.)Within three working days after submitting an application for an adjustable-rate mortgage loan, which disclosure is considered necessary? A.) The CHARM booklet

B.) The Loan Estimate

C.) The Home Loan Tool Kit booklet

D.) All of the above

84.) If a house is valued by an appraiser at $200,000 and the homeowner qualifies for a new cash-out refinance for 90% LTV, how much cash can they pull out if they currently have a first mortgage of $60,000; a second mortgage of $20,000; and $5,000 in closing costs which are financed into the loan?

A.) $88,000

B.) $90,000

C.) $93,000

D.) $95,000

85.) Except for what fee, can a mortgage loan originator collect any fees from an application before presenting them with a Loan Estimate?

A.) An appraisal fee

B.) An application fee

C.) A credit report fee

D.) None of the above

86.) Which type of security instrument lets the mortgagor convey an interest in property to the mortgage as collateral for the debt, thus creating a voluntary lien on the property?

A.) Title

B.) Deed

C.) Sales contract

D.) Mortgage

87.) What should a loan officer do if an applicant refuses to give ethnic, racial, or gender information on an in-person application?

A.) Leave the information blank and continue with the application

B.) Keep in mind that the data was gathered based on visual observation or surname

C.) Notify the borrower that the information is required by law

D.) None of the above

88.) What is the phrase used for accumulated interest since the previous month's payment?

A.) Adjustable-rate interest

B.) Per diem interest

C.) Accrued interest

D.) Monthly interest

89.) Which of the following is subject to a zero-tolerance for change when comparing the Closing Disclosure to the Loan Estimate?

A.) Settlement agent fees

B.) Government recording fees

C.) Lender application fees

D.) Pest inspection fees

90.) What do you call the name of the clause in a note payable that allows a lender to declare the entire loan sum due immediately if a borrower defaults or breaks other contract terms?

A.) Acceleration

B.) Re-conveyance

C.) Termination

D.) Safe harbor provisions

91.) Regulation B implements what law?

A.) HMDA

B.) RESPA

C.) ECOA

D.) TILA

92.) When does a consumer become contractually bound to a credit transaction?

A.) At settlement

B.) At consummation

C.) At the signing of the sales contract

D.) None of the above

93.) Which of the following does not necessitate licensee notification to the NMLS and the state regulatory authority?

A.) Having a civil lawsuit filed against them for damaging property

B.) Getting charged with arson

C.) Filing for bankruptcy

D.) Having your mortgage license revoked in another state

94.) Which of the following does Regulation C implement?

A.) RESPA

B.) ECOA

C.) HMDA

D.) FCRA

95.) If a homeowner takes out a $113,000 loan, and the annual interest is $6,215, what is the interest rate on this loan?

A.) 4.75%

B.) 5.00%

C.) 5.25%

D.) 5.50%

96.) Which government agency assists in the provision of mortgage loans to low-income borrowers in rural areas?

A.) The Department of Housing and Urban Development

B.) The United States Department of Agriculture

C.) The Federal Housing Administration

D.) The Government National Mortgage Association

97.) For how long does title insurance safeguard the title?

A.) since the initial registration of the property through the time of closing

B.) For the seven years preceding the deadline

C.) From the time of the property's closure until the next transfer of title

D.) None of the above

. . .

98.) For escrow accounts created as a condition of the loan, a loan servicer must give the borrower their initial escrow account statement within how many calendar days of settlement?

A.) Seven days

B.) 15 days

C.) 30 days

D.) 45 days

99.) Which of the following mortgage programs requires a one-time mortgage insurance premium?

A.) FHA mortgages

B.) Veterans Administration Loans

C.) Expensive mortgages

D.) Subprime loans

PRACTICE TEST 1 ANSWERS

ANSWERS

1.) RESPA aids in the regulation of which of the following?

The correct answer is: B - Kickbacks

RESPA is primarily concerned with kickbacks, which is a type of illegal compensation given to a loan originator, real estate agent, or other service provider for referring business to another party.

2.) Within how many working days of receipt a loan application should the Good Faith Estimate or Loan Estimate be given to a borrower??

The correct answer is: A - 3 business days. The Good Faith Estimate or Loan Estimate must be sent to an applicant within 3 business days of receiving a loan application.

3.) Red Flags Rule extends instructions for?

The correct answer is: D-Identity theft. The Red Flags Rule provides warning signs of identity theft and requires financial institutions to have written programs in place to identify and prevent identity theft.

4.) A mortgage is considered high cost under the Home Ownership and Equity Protection Act (HOEPA) if the total points and fees exceed what % of the loan amount?

The correct answer is: A - 5%. A high-cost mortgage is a first mortgage with an APR that exceeds the APR by 6.5 percent, a second mortgage with an APR that exceeds the APR by 8.5 percent, or a loan that has total points and fees that exceed 5 percent of the amount borrowed.

5.) On which timeframe should the borrower receive the Affiliated Business Arrangement disclosure?

The correct answer is: D- At or before the time of the referral. The Affiliated Business Arrangement disclosure has to be given to the borrower at or before the time of the referral if there is more than 1% common ownership between the businesses. The dis- closure should explain the relationship between the companies along with the charges for the company the buyer is being referred to.

6.) After conducting an analysis of escrow accounts, how much must an escrow account be overpaid by to allow the borrower to get a refund?

The correct answer is: A - $50. If the borrower has paid at least $50 over the amount needed to pay for escrow bills when the lender completes the Annual Escrow Analysis Statement, the borrower must be refunded the amount they overpaid.

7.) Once a borrower's loan has been fully paid off, what will they be issued?

The correct answer is: B- A discharge of mortgage. Once a loan has been paid off, a mortgage discharge will be recorded with the Registry of Deeds, and the title to the home will be free and clear.

8.) What does the ECOA entitle consumers to receive a copy of?

A - The property appraisal report is the correct answer. ECOA requires lenders to produce a copy of the property appraisal report "promptly" (i.e., within three business days of the appraisal's completion) or at least three business days before the loan closes.

9.) Which of the following things may lenders use to determine loan eligibility?

The correct answer is: D- Credit-worthiness. The Equal Credit Opportunity Act bans lenders from using certain characteristics to determine loan eligibility. These include ethnicity, color, religion, national origin, sex, marital status, age, and receipt of public assistance.

10.)Which of these describes an affiliated business relationship that must be disclosed?

The right solution is: C- A lender who owns a stake in a settlement firm that conducts the closing on one of their deals for a fee. When a lender owns more than 1% of an affiliated business or has a personal stake in the provider, RESPA requires the lender to provide an Affiliated Business Agreement disclosure. Before or at the time of the referral, the customer must be given the Affiliated Business Arrangement Disclosure Form.

11.) Which of these transactions doesn't allow the borrower a Right to Rescind?

The correct answer is: B- A purchase loan The Right of Rescission applies to all refinances, HELOCs, and home equity loans. It does not apply to purchase loans.

12.)After receiving a loan application, how many working days should the statement of Mortgage Servicing Disclosure be delivered to the borrower?

C-3 working days is the right answer. The statement of the Mortgage Servicing Disclosure should be given to the borrower no later than one day after the loan application is received.

13.) Which one of the following is authorized by the Home Mortgage Disclosure Act (HMDA)?

The correct answer is: D- All of the above. The Home Mortgage Disclosure Act demands that financial institutions maintain and report certain information about mortgages, including the loan amount, property location, and the race of the borrower, along with other information.

14.) Which law stipulates financial institutions to post privacy advisories and to protect customers' personal information

The correct answer is: C- The Gramm-Leach Bliley Act. The Gramm-Leach-Bliley Act includes the Financial Privacy Rule, which regulates how financial institutions collect and disclose private financial information.

15.) Among the following, which one is a function of the FACTA?

The right solution is: A - It empowers customers to a free credit disclose once a year.

Consumers are entitled to one complimentary credit disclose from each of the credit reporting agencies each year under the Act. It also prevents identity theft by allowing consumers to set credit report alerts if they feel their identification has been stolen

16.) How many billing cycles must the Special Information Booklet be delivered to a borrower following obtaining a loan request?

The correct answer is: B-3 business days. The Special Information Booklet must be delivered to a customer within 3 working days of receipt of a loan application.

17.) What should a loan originator do if a loan applicant refuses to reveal their ethnicity?

The correct answer is: C-Make a prediction based on visual observations is the right answer. If a loan applicant refuses to reveal their ethnicity, the loan originator should make a best guess based on visual observations and fill in the application.

18.) How many days after getting a Loan Estimate must an applicant indicate purpose to Continue?

The correct answer is: B-10 days. A borrower must indicate purpose to go ahead within 10 business days of receiving a Loan Estimate. If they wish to move forward after 10 days, the terms of the loan may change.

19.)How many hours of pre-licensing instruction is required for a loan originator to become licensed?

The correct answer is: D- 20 hours. National pre-licensing courses require 20 hours of education that includes three hours worth of federal law, three hours worth of ethics, two hours of non-traditional mortgage product content, and lastly, twelve hours of elective information.

20.) How frequently must MLOs renew their licenses?

The correct answer is: A- Every year. Loan originators must renew their licenses and fulfill continuing education requirements each year. The period for submitting an application for MLO license renewal is from November 1 through December 31.

21.) Within how many days of receiving a complete application, lenders should notify clients of any adverse action taken?

B-30 days is the correct answer. Creditors must notify applicants of their credit status and the reasons for any adverse action taken within 30 days of receiving the application.

22.) To what law does Regulation V apply?

The right response is D, which stands for the Fair Credit Reporting Act.

23.) Which of the following is the mortgagor?

The borrower is the proper response. A borrower is referred to as a mortgagor, and a lender is referred to as a mortgagee.

24.) What are the different types of liens that come with getting a mortgage?

A - A voluntary lien is the correct answer. A voluntary lien is used to secure a mortgage.

25.) What date determines an alien's position?

The correct response is B- the recording date. The alien's position is determined by the date and time of recording.

26.) When the customer receives revised disclosures before closing on a fixed-rate loan, how much variance in the APR is required?

The correct answer is: A- 1/8th of a percent is the correct answer. If there is a change of more than 1/8th of a percent to the APR for a regular transaction (generally, a fixed-rate loan) or a change greater than 1/4th of a percent to the APR for an irregular transaction, the Mortgage Disclosure Improvement Act need redisclosure and a three-day waiting interval after the customer gets the amended disclosures before finalizing (generally, an adjustable-rate loan).

27.) After the first mortgage lien, what phrase is used to represent liens that are recorded?

C- Junior Liens is the right answer. A lien that is created after the first one has been recorded.

A junior lien is one that is attached to a mortgage.

28.) Which of the following statements concerning FHA loans is correct?

FHA mortgages are insured, hence the right answer is A. The Federal Housing Administration insures FA mortgages (FHA).

29.) To compute the fully indexed rate on an adjustable-rate mortgage once it starts to adjust, which of the following two must be added together?

B- The margin and the Index is the correct answer. The fully indexed rate is obtained by putting the margin and index together. The margin is a predetermined amount that is used to cover the lender's costs and profit. The index is a fluctuating, verifiable reported rate.

30.) What is the maximum interest rate for the second adjustment period of a 15-year ARM with a beginning interest rate of 3.75 percent, an adjustment rate cap of 2.25 percent, and a lifetime ceiling of 9 percent?

D- 8.25 percent is the right answer. The adjustment rate cap specifies the maximum amount of adjustment that can be made. In one adjustment period, the interest rate can rise. As an example, if a 15-year ARM had a 3.75 percent starting interest rate and a 2.25 percent adjustment rate cap, you would add the two to get the highest rate of interest for the next adjustment period and then another 2.25 for the second period of adjustment (in this case, 8.25 percent).

31.) What is the name for the act of transferring ownership, right, title, or interests in a property from one entity to another?

B-Conveyance is the right answer. The act of transferring ownership, right, title, and interests in a property from one entity to another is known as conveyance.

32.) When does the rescission period for an owner-occupied refinance deal subject to the Regulation Z right of recession expire if the transaction closes on a Monday, assuming no federal holidays throughout the week?

Thursday is the correct answer. Consumers can exercise their right to rescind for agreements subject to the Regulation Z right of recession until the third business day following loan completion, delivery of the requisite rescission notification, or delivery of all material disclosures, whichever comes first. The rescission time ends on Thursday in this case. On Friday, the money flows and the loan is funded, and the transaction is complete.

33.) Which of the following mortgages would require private mortgage insurance (PMI)?

A - A conventional loan with a 16 percent down payment is the correct answer.

For traditional loans with a down payment of less than 20%, private mortgage insurance (PMI) is required. When the loan-to-value ratio reaches 80 percent, the borrower cancels PMI, and when it reaches 78 percent, the lender cancels it.

34.) What is the meaning of PITI?

D - Principal, interest, taxes, and insurance is the right answer. Principal, interest, taxes, and insurance are all acronyms for principal, interest, taxes, and insurance. The major components of a borrower's monthly payment are these.

35.) In a gift letter, which of the following must be included?

The correct answer is: D- All of the above. The donor's name and address are included in a gift letter. The gift's value, the recipient's dress, and a note that the gift is not refundable.

36.) For a $350,000 loan, how much does a 2 and a half discount point cost?

C- $8,750 is the correct answer. Each discount point is worth 1% of the total loan amount. To determine the cost of two 12-point discount points, multiply the loan amount of $350,000 by .025 to get $8,750.

37.) How much interest would the borrower owe for the days remaining in the month if a $300,000 loan with a 7% interest rate is closed on a property with a purchase price of $340,000 and there are 8 days left in the month?

C- $460.27 is the right answer. The interest for the remaining days in the month is calculated by multiplying the loan amount by the interest rate, dividing by 365 days to get the daily value, then multiplying the daily value by the number of days left in the month, which is 8. As a result, 300,000 x.07 divided by 365, multiplied by 8 equals $460.27.

38.) For a home with a purchase price of $250,000, an appraisal of $240,000, and an LTV ratio of 80%, what is the loan amount?

The right answer is B, which equals $192,000. The loan-to-value ratio is computed by dividing the loan amount by the purchase price or appraised value, whichever is lower. So, in this case, we'd take the appraised value of $240,000 and divide it by 80 percent to get $192,000.

39.) With a $1920 PITI payment, a $240 condo fee, and a gross monthly income of $9,600, what would the housing expense ratio be?

D -22.50 percent is the right answer. The PITI payment is divided by the borrower's gross monthly income to calculate the housing expense ratio. As a result, 2,160 / 9,600 = 0.2250, or 22.5 percent.

40.) What is a homeowners total monthly income if they work 50 hours a week and earn $15 per hour?

The correct answer is: C- $3,250. The borrower's gross monthly income can be calculated by multiplying their hourly rate by the number of hours they work per week, then multiplying that by 52 weeks, and then dividing that by 12 months to get $3,250

41.) What is the late charge fee for a borrower with a VA (veterans affairs) loan of $400,000, monthly P&I of $1,600, annual PMI of $1,850, annual hazard insurance of $2,500, and annual property taxes of $ 3,800?

The correct answer is: B- $64. Late fees for VA loans are 4 percent. They are calculated by multiplying the monthly principal and interest amount by 4 percent, which would be 1,600 x.04, which equals $64.

42.) What is the minimum number of years of job experience required on a loan application?

A - 2 years is the correct answer. On a loan application, a borrower is usually required to furnish two years of employment history.

43.) When calculating monthly debt based on information from a credit report, what proportion of the total is used if no minimum monthly credit card payment is stated?

The correct answer is: A - 5% If you don't have a minimum monthly credit card payment, the lender can estimate the monthly payment by computing 5% of the remaining balance based on the applicant's credit record.

44.) Do bankruptcies stay on a person's credit report for a long time?

The correct answer is: C- 10 years. Bankruptcies can be held on a person's record for a long time. For a period of up to ten years, your credit report will be kept on file.

45.) For a single-borrower loan, what is the indicative credit rating if the lender obtains two credit-worthiness?

The correct answer is: B- The lower of the two Scores. When a lender receives two credit scores for a single borrower loan, the representative credit score is the lower of the two scores.

46.) If the closing date is August 21, when is the first mortgage payment due?

The correct answer is: A- October 1st. The first payment is not required until the loan is closed until the second month following the date of closing. As a result, if a loan closes in June, the first payment isn't due until August 1st.

47.) Who is qualified to receive a real estate broker's referral fee?

The correct answer is: B - Other real estate broker referral fees are paid by real estate brokers to other real estate brokerage businesses.

48.) What is the most prevalent type of mortgage fraud?

Equity skimming is the correct answer. Equity skimming is a kind of mortgage fraud which includes inflating an appraisal in order for the borrower or refinancer to pocket extra money.

49.) What is the acronym for APR?

The right answer is B, which stands for "average prime offer rate." The average prime offer rate is abbreviated as APR. This is the average annual percentage rate

(APR) for low-risk loans with similar points and conditions.

50.) A loan given to a low-credit creditor is referred to by which of the following terms?

C- Subprime is the right answer. It's one that's made available to a bad-credit borrower.

51.) What kind of financial crime involves a group of culprits applying for a mortgage with a fictitious borrower and assets?

The correct answer is: A-Air loans. Air loans are a sort of mortgage fraud in which a group of criminals apply for a loan using a fictitious borrower and property.

52.)What loan-to-value ratio permits the lender's obligation for private mortgage insurance (PMII) to be canceled?

The correct answer is: D- 78%. The lender must cancel private mortgage insurance when it reaches 78 percent (PMI).

53.) Which of the relevant documentation may a salaried employee be required to provide in order to obtain a loan?

The correct answer is: C- W-2s Salaried employees are usually required to present W-2s from the previous two years as verification of income.

54.)What forms of loans are available for rural properties?

The correct answer is: B- USDA loans. The United States Department of Agriculture

(USDA) offers loans to low-income families for properties that are located in rural areas.

55.) Which term describes a property's increase in value?

The correct answer is: A- Appreciation is the growth in the value of a property owing to modifications or market appreciation.

56.) How long are credit reports valid once they've been pulled for qualification purposes?

The correct answer is: D- 120 days. After being issued, credit reports are valid for 120 days pulled for the purpose of qualification.

57.) The FBI identifies two types of mortgage fraud. What are they?

The correct answer is D - Profit and housing fraud. The FBI has identified two categories of mortgage fraud: profit fraud and housing fraud. Fraud for profit indicates the offenders are looking to make money, whereas fraud for housing means they are looking for a place to live.

58.) A purchaser will not buy more for one asset than for another of equivalent value, according to which of the following hypothesis?

The correct answer is B- The Substitution Principle. A buyer won't pay more for one property than they would for another of equivalent value, according to the principle of substitution.

59.)In what type of mortgage fraud is a borrower who has no intention of repaying the loan?

The correct answer is: A- Fictitious loans. A fictitious loan is a type of mortgage scam with a borrower who does not intend to repay the debt. They frequently utilize a stolen or made-up identity.

60.) What of the following is a sign of mortgage fraud?

The correct answer is: D- All of the above. Changes between a handwritten and typed application, a borrower buying an investment property without having a primary residence, and verifications conducted on a holiday or weekend are all warning flags that could indicate mortgage fraud.

61.) Which of the following forms is used to verify information about a job?

The correct answer is: B- Verification of Employment. Fannie Mae 1005, or the Verification of Employment, must be filled out by the applicant's employer to verify employment.

62.) What is the alternative name for Fannie Mae's automated underwriting system?

A- Desktop Underwriter is the correct answer.

63.) Which of the following words describes the most likely price at which an asset will be sold on the open market?

C-Market value is the right answer. A property's market value is the most likely price at which it will sell on the open market.

64.) What is the most often utilized residential appraisal method?

The correct answer is: A - Market Approach. The Market Approach is most commonly used for residential properties. It compares a property to at least three sold properties with similar characteristics.

65.)Using the Income Method, what is a property's value with a $50,000 annual net operating income and a 9% capitalization rate?

The correct answer is: A- $555,555.56. The Income Approach calculates property value by dividing the annual net operating income by the capitalization rate. In this example we would use 50,000 / .09 which equals $555,555.56

66.) Which organization handles mortgage refusal complaints?

The correct answer is: C- CFPB. The Consumer Financial Protection Bureau deals

with complaints about consumer financial products and services.

67.)Which of the following permits someone other than the owner of the property to be on the property for a particular reason?

The correct answer is: A- An easement. An easement gives an individual other than the property owner the right to be on the property for a distinct reason.

68.) Which one of the following guidelines refers to a property's most profitable and acceptable use?

The correct answer is: C - The Principle of Highest and Best Use The Principle of Highest and Best Use is the most promising use for a property that is legally permissible, physically possible, and financially feasible.

69.) What term is used to describe a claim on a property that may limit its ability to be sold?

D-A title defect is the correct answer. A title deficiency makes it difficult to sell a home. This could affect the borrower's right to own the property after closing. Undiscovered liens, fraudulent paperwork, undeclared heirs, and recording errors are all examples of title flaws.

70.) What is the phrase for when a lender sells a mortgage to another lender?

The correct answer is: B- Assignment of mortgage.

71.) If a loan broker wants the customer's consent to obtain copies of their tax returns of their income, the prospective customer must sign what form?

The correct answer is: A. Form 4506-T gives the lender consent to obtain copies of a prospective borrower's income tax returns.

72.) Which lien is paid firstly during a foreclosure sale?

The correct answer is: C- The property tax lien Property tax liens are always paid first when a property is foreclosed and sold.

73.) If a lender refuses to give security-backed loans in a certain neighborhood due to the ethnic or racial design of the area, they are committing the prohibited act of?

The correct answer is: B-Redlining. Redlining is a prohibited practice under the Fair Housing Act where a lender refuses to make loans on property located in a specific neighborhood due to reasons such as the racial or ethnic composition of the neighborhood; effectively drawing a red line around an area that they do not wish to do business in.

74.) If a mortgage advertisement implies a rate of finance charge, how must it state the rate?

The correct answer is: B- The APR. If the advertisement states any interest rate or finance charge, the consumer must also be provided the annual percentage rate in the advertisement.

75.) Of the following choices, which expense associated with a home loan is NOT paid from an escrow account?

The correct answer is: A - Title fees. On the insurance of homeowners, taxes of assets, and hazard insurance are typically costs whose payments are made right out of an escrow account attached to the mortgage loan.

76.) According to the Equal Credit Opportunity Act, which of the following sources of income may be eliminated for the purpose of qualifying the borrower's income??

The correct answer is: C- Short-term disability. The Equal Credit Opportunity Act sets forth that all legal sources of regular income must be considered, providing that the income will continue for an acceptable length of time.

77.) The interest rate estimate provided on a Loan Estimate must be available for at least how many working days after the applicant is awarded the loan.

The correct answer is: D-None of the above. While the estimate for most settlement charges must be available for at least 10 business days, no restrictions are present on the amount of time that the interest rate must remain available.

78.)What type of mortgage fraud has an applicant committed if he purposefully withholds information that would preclude him from acquiring a mortgage loan?

The correct answer is: A- Omission.

79.) If a borrower makes $4300 in gross monthly income, what is the maximum "total" debt allowed for them by a conventional lender?

The correct answer is: B- $1,720. Conventional lenders want the borrower's housing expenses plus other recurring monthly debt to not exceed 40% of their monthly income. So in this case we would multiply the gross monthly income of $4300 by .40 to get $1,720, which is the maximum total debt allowed under that gross monthly income.

80.) Which of the following fees would NOT be considered a finance charge in the APR calculation?

The correct answer is: D - Escrow deposit for hazard insurance. Escrow deposits are never included in the calculation of the APR. The APR, unlike an interest rate, includes charges or fees such as mortgage insurance, most closing costs, discount points, and loan origination fees.

81). If a homeowner "buy's down" the interest rate on their loan, how would that reflect on the Loan Estimate?

The right answer is: D- A charge to the borrower. A buydown is a fee applied to the borrower, which is paid at closing on the Loan Estimate as a charge to the borrower.

82.) What is the age requirement for a reverse mortgage borrower?

The correct answer is: C- 62. C- A reverse mortgage is only available to those who are at least 62 years old.

83.)Within three working days after submitting an application for an adjustable-rate mortgage loan, which disclosure is considered necessary?

A- The CHARM pamphlet is the correct solution. Lenders issuing residential mortgages for ARM loans must comply with Regulation Z and give those loan applicants with the Consumer pamphlet on Adjustable Rate Mortgages within 3 business days.

84.) If a house is valued by an appraiser at $200,000 and the homeowner qualifies for a new cash-out refinance for 90% LTV, how much cash can they pull out if they currently have a first mortgage of $60,000; a second mortgage of $20,000; and $5,000 in closing costs which are financed into the loan?

The correct answer is: D- $95,000. To calculate the amount of cash that can be pulled out, first determine the maximum loan amount by multiplying the appraised value of $200,000 by the maximum loan to value of 85% to get $172,000. Then subtract the balances of the first mortgage, the second mortgage along with the closing cost to get the cash out amount of $95,000.

85.) Except for what fee, can a mortgage loan originator collect any fees from an application before presenting them with a Loan Estimate?

C-A credit report cost is the right answer.. The TILA RESPA Integrated Disclosure rule, TRID, sets forth that no fee, with the exclusion of an authentic and reasonable credit report charge, may be acquired by a mortgage loan originator or lender up till when the borrower has received the initial application disclosures, including the Loan Estimate and the loan originator or lender has acknowledged the borrower's intent to proceed with the mortgage loan.

86.) Which type of security instrument lets the mortgagor convey an interest in property to the mortgage as collateral for the debt, thus creating a voluntary lien on the property?

The correct answer is: D- Mortgage. A mortgage is a type of security instrument. When a borrower (mortgagor) transfers an interest in real estate to a lender (mortgagee) as collateral for a debt, the lender (mortgagee) creates a voluntary lien on the property.

87.) What should a loan officer do if an applicant refuses to give ethnic, racial, or gender information on an in-person application?

The correct answer is: B- Note that the information was collected on the basis on sensory observation or surname. If the applicant decides not to tell their ethnicity, race or gender, then the loan officer must identify the applicant's ethnicity, race, and gender based on sensory observation or their sur- name. The lender must also notate that the applicant's ethnicity, race, and/or sex were collected on the basis of sensory observation or surname.

88.) What is the phrase used for accumulated interest since the previous month's payment?

C- Accrued interest is the right answer. The interest on a loan that has accrued since the main investment or the prior payment is referred to as accrued interest.

89.) Which of the following is subject to a zero-tolerance for change when comparing the Closing Disclosure to the Loan Estimate?

From the Loan Estimate through the Closing Disclosure, transfer taxes, as well as any charges paid to the lender, mortgage broker, or their affiliates for the processing, origination, and closing of a mortgage loan, must not vary.

90.) What do you call the name of the clause in a note payable that allows a lender to declare the entire loan sum due immediately if a borrower defaults or breaks other contract terms?

A- Acceleration is the correct answer. The acceleration clause is a note payable that gives a lender the authority to declare the entire loan balance due immediately if certain conditions are met, i.e. when the borrower defaults or violates other contract provisions.

91.) Regulation B implements what law?

The correct answer is: C- ECOA. Equal Credit Opportunity Act (ECOA).

92.) When does a consumer become contractually bound to a credit transaction?

B- It occurs at consummation. This is not the case for a customer, however.

93.) Which of the following does not necessitate licensee notification to the NMLS and the state regulatory authority?

A- Being charged with a misdemeanor is the right answer.

94.) Which of the following does Regulation C implement?

The correct answer is: C- HMDA. Regulation C is the vehicle through which the Home Mortgage Disclosure Act is put into effect.

95). If a homeowner takes out a $113,000 loan, and the annual interest is $6,215, what is the interest rate on this loan?

The correct answer is: D-5.50%. To compute the interest rate using the loan amount and annual interest, you divide the annual interest amount of $6,215 into the loan amount of $113,000 to get .055 or 5.5%

96.) Which government agency assists in the provision of mortgage loans to low-income borrowers in rural areas?

The right solution is: The Department of Agriculture (Department B). The United States Department of Agriculture offers rural Americans homeownership opportunities as well as house remodeling and repair programs. In multi-unit housing complexes, the USDA also provides finance to elderly, disabled, or low-income rural residents to ensure that they are able to make rent payments.

97). For how long does title insurance safeguard the title?

The correct response is: A- From the time of the property's first registration to the time of closing. From the time the land was originally registered until the time of closure, title insurance protects the title. It safeguards the title exam against flaws and the closing from mistakes.

98.) For escrow accounts created as a condition of the loan, a loan servicer must provide the borrower with an initial escrow account statement within how many calendar days of settlement?

D- 45 days is the correct answer. For escrow accounts established as a condition of the loan, RESPA mandates 45 days of settlement.

99.) Which of the following mortgage programs requires a one-time mortgage insurance premium?

A-FHA loans is the correct answer. An upfront mortgage insurance fee is required for FHA loans. There is a funding cost on VA loans, but no upfront mortgage insurance premium.

MATH PRACTICE TEST (19 QUESTIONS)

Answers Follow After Q19.

----

1. Jane is 48 years old. Her desire is to buy a home where she will need to bring $500,000 as a downpayment. She wants to use her retirement savings in her IRA, which is valued at $612,200. If Jane satisfies all of other closing conditions, will she be able to close using IRA if they are the only funds she has?

2) James intends to buy a home valued at $200000. This will equal an LTV of 85. The Lender has asked him to pay $7000 in "discount points ."How many discount points will he pay for?

3) How much will a purchaser's settlement expenses be reduced if she chooses an above-par interest rate

that results in a 5% closing cost credit, assuming a purchase price of $600,000 and a 30% down payment?

4) How much money will Linda spend on discount points if she buys a house for $ 300,000 with a 30% down payment and 3.5 discount points?

5) A purchaser buys a home for $600,000 and puts 40% as a down-payment. How much is their down payment?

6) An applicant gets $30 per hour and usually works 40 hours per week. How much money does the applicant make each month?

7) In the first adjustment period of an 5/1 Adjustable Rate Mortgage (with a cap structure of 5/2/5 and a starting rate of 2.5 percent), what rate would the purchaser's interest advance to if the index becomes 4 with a margin of 5?

8) If a property is worth $500,000 and the borrower has a first mortgage of $200,000 and a second mortgage of $95,000, what is the LTV and CLTV?

9) Fred uses a down payment of 11%. By using piggy bank funding, he wants to avoid private mortgage insurance payments. How has he come to this calculation?

10) If a purchaser earns $80,000 per year and his housing expense is $6,000, what is his house expense ratio?

11) The P&I for a buyer is monthly $3,000, which includes $7,000 in annual real estate taxes in Escrow, insurance amounting to $1,800 yearly, and a monthly PMI of $60 in monthly PMI. What is the monthly PITI payment?

12) If a consumer's monthly salary is $10,000. His monthly non-housing-related expenses are $2000, and his back-end DTI is 55%. How much does his housing cost in total?

13) On the tenth calendar day of the month, a $340,000 conventional mortgage obligation is due. If the current month's payment was credited on the 6th and the loan has a per diem of $19.50, what is the total payoff?

14) Brianna works as a caregiver earning $53 per hour. She works 40 hours each week and gets remunerated bi-weekly. What is her gross bi-weekly payment?

15) An asset is worth $700,000. There is a 60 percent CLTV on both the first and second mortgages. 20% for the LTV of the second mortgage. What is the amount overdue on your first mortgage?

16) Boris has an income of $2000 per month in social security disability which is untaxed. With what amount do you credit her?

17) A buyer buys a property with a 2-1 buydown guarantee. The note rate of the consumer gives a payment of $4500. How much money did the 2-1 buydown cost the seller if the client then needed to pay a P&I payment of $2,230 in year one and $2,350 in year two?

- $10,146
- $30000
- $26,000
- $53,040

18) Jason's loan amount is $170,000 on a $320,000 buying price. How much percentage was his purchase price, and how much was his down payment, in dollars?

- $150,000/47
- $110,000/30
- $125,000/50
- $160,000/53

19) A prospect wishes to spend $700,000 on a property. He has $70,000 to put down as downpayment, however he wants to avoid PMI. How would you go about financing this transaction using piggy bank financing?

- Mortgage insurance cannot be avoided
- A first mortgage for $640,000 after the $65000 down payment

- A first mortgage for $490,000 with a second mortgage for $70,000
- A first mortgage for $600,000 and a second mortgage for $50,000

MATH PRACTICE TEST - ANSWERS

----

1) Jane is 48 years old. Her desire is to buy a home where she will need to bring $500,000 as a downpayment. She wants to use her retirement savings in her IRA, which is valued at $612,200. If Jane satisfies all of other closing conditions, will she be able to close using IRA if they are the only funds she has?

Solution

To use the retirement funds as a source of settlement funds when your age is less than 59 ½, then the amount of retirement savings in any specific retirement account should equate to or exceed 20% of the amount of money required to close. Each of these accounts are considered at 70% of the face value. Jane is younger than 59 ½ and so $428,400 which is 70% of $612,000 is available for her use. Hence Jane will need to top up or prove ownership of an extra $71,600 ($500000-428,400) in order to close on the home.

2) James intends to buy a home valued at $200000. This will equal an LTV of 85. The Lender has asked him to pay $7000 in "discount points." How many discount points will he pay for?

Solution

Purchase price =$200000

LTV =85% = $(85*200000)/100 =$170,000

Points are calculated based on the loan amount.

1 point =0.01 of the loan amount =$(0.01*170000)=$1700

Therefore $7000=>$7000/$170000=0.04=>4 points

3) How much will a purchaser's settlement expenses be reduced if she chooses an above-par interest rate that results in a 5% closing cost credit, assuming a purchase price of $600,000 and a 30% down payment?

Solution

With a 30% down payment, the loan amount would be

30% of $600000 = $180000

$600000 - 180000 = $420,000

If the rate generates a 5% cost credit, the purchaser will receive

$420000 * 3% = $13600

4) How much money will Linda spend on discount points if she buys a house for $ 300,000 with a 30% down payment and 3.5 discount points?

Solution

Purchase price = $300000

Discount points cost = $(3.5 * 210,000)/100 = $7350

5) A purchaser buys a home for $600,000 and puts 40% as a down-payment. How much is their down payment?

Solution

Down payment = $600,000 *40% = $240,000

6) An applicant gets $30 per hour and usually works 40 hours per week. How much money does the applicant make each month?

Solution

Weekly rate = $30*40 = $1200

Because a year has 52 weeks, the weekly rate is multiplied by 52 to get the annual income.

$62,400= 52*1200

After that, the annual income is divided by 12 to get the monthly income.

$62,400/12 =$5200. Note, you cannot simply multiple $1200 by 4 weeks in a month, as this would give a different and incorrect answer ($4800).

7) In the first adjustment period of an 5/1 Adjustable Rate Mortgage (with a cap structure of 5/2/5 and a starting rate of 2.5 percent), what rate would the purchaser's interest advance to if the index becomes 4 with a margin of 5?

Solution

If there was no cap, the rate would climb from 2.5% to 9% (index+margin= full indexed accrual rate [FIAR]). The borrower's rate can only go up to 7.5 percent because the loan has a 5 percent first adjustment cap.

8) If a property is worth $500,000 and the borrower has a first mortgage of $200,000 and a second mortgage of $95,000, what is the LTV and CLTV?

Solution

LTV= (200,000/500000)*100% = 40%

CLTV = Sum total of the two debts/property value

(200,000+95,000)/500,000 = 0.79*100% =79%

9) Fred uses a down payment of 11%. By using piggy bank funding, he wants to avoid private mortgage insurance payments. How has he come to this calculation?

65/15/20

Solution

When constructing a piggy bank scenario, the first number is always the primary mortgage's LTV. Because the primary purpose is to avoid paying PMI, the loan must be under 80%. The second figure is the second mortgage's LTV, and the third number is the borrower's down payment (20 percent). Because LTV+Equity must always equal 100 percent, all three values must add up to 100 percent.

10) If a purchaser earns $80,000 per year and his housing expense is $6,000, what is his house expense ratio?

Solution

Income of the buyer monthly = yearly income/12 months

=$80,000/12= $6,667

expense of housing ratio = expense of housing income monthly

=6000/6667 =9%

11) The P&I for a buyer is monthly $3,000, which includes $7,000 in annual real estate taxes in Escrow, insurance amounting to $1,800 yearly, and a monthly PMI of $60 in monthly PMI. What is the monthly PITI payment?

Solution

Insurance and taxes on property are paid on an annual basis. When you add them together and divide the total by 12, you get a monthly equivalency.

(7,000 + 1,800 = 8,800/12 = 733.33.)

Then, when you add the monthly P&I of $3,000 and the monthly PMI of $60, you get a monthly PITI of $2,596.67.

$3,793.33 = $733.33 + $3,000 + $60

12) If a consumer's monthly salary is $10,000. His monthly non-housing-related expenses are $2000, and his back-end DTI is 55%. How much does his housing cost in total?

Solution

If the total of all expenses (back-end ratio) equals 25% of the buyer's gross monthly income

10,000*0.55 = $5500

Of that, $2000 is monthly expenses. His housing expenses would be equal to $5500. Then, $5500 - $2000 = $3500.

13) On the tenth calendar day of the month, a $340,000 conventional mortgage obligation is due. If the current month's payment was credited on the 6th and the loan has a per diem of $19.50, what is the total payoff?

Solution

If the balance owed on the 1st of the month is $295,000 and the loan payoff 5 days later, 5 additional days of interest are due. Since

$19.50*6 = $117

Final payoff = $340,000 + $117 = $340,117

14) Brianna works as a caregiver earning $53 per hour. She works 40 hours each week and gets remunerated bi-weekly. What is her gross bi-weekly payment?

Solution

Weekly rate =$53*40= $2,120

Annual rate =2120*52=$110,240

A year has 52 weeks, and because she is paid bi-weekly, we divide 52/2 which is 26 weeks.

Bi-weekly payment = $110240/26=$4,240

15) An asset is worth $700,000. There is a 60 percent CLTV on both the first and second mortgages. 20% for the LTV of the second mortgage. What is the amount overdue on your first mortgage?

Solution

First and second mortgages constitute 60% of the assets facevalue. The second mortgage constitutes 20%.

So the first mortgage consists = 60%-20%=40%

First mortgage balance =40%*700,000=$280,000

16) Boris has an income of $2000 per month in social security disability which is untaxed. With what amount do you credit her?

Solution

In such a case where social security disability income is untaxed, you may increase by 25%

2000*25%=500

2000+500=$2,500

17) A buyer buys a property with a 2-1 buydown guarantee. The note rate of the consumer gives a payment of $4500. How much money did the 2-1 buydown cost the seller if the client then needed to pay a P&I payment of $2,230 in year one and $2,350 in year two?

- $10,146
- $30000
- $26,000
- $53,040

Solution

Answer: D

If the customer remits $2230 for the first year, he is saving $2270 monthly.

4500-2230 = $2270

If the customer remits $2350 for the second year, he is saving $2150monthly

4500-2350 = 2150

So when twelve payments of

2270*12 = 27240

2150*12 =25800

are added together, the seller will spend $53040 to fund the 2-1 buydown.

18) Jason's loan amount is $170,000 on a $320,000 buying price. How much percentage was his purchase price, and how much was his down payment, in dollars?

- $150,000/47

- $110,000/30
- $125,000/50
- $160,000/53

Solution

Answer: A

Down payment = purchase price - loan amount

$320,000-$170,000= $150,000

Down payment of $150,000 divided by $320,000 buying price = 46.9%=47%

19) A prospect wishes to spend $700,000 on a property. He has $70,000 to put down as downpayment, however he wants to avoid PMI. How would you go about financing this transaction using piggy bank financing?

- Mortgage insurance cannot be avoided
- A first mortgage for $640,000 after the $65000 down payment
- A first mortgage for $490,000 with a second mortgage for $70,000
- A first mortgage for $600,000 and a second mortgage for $50,000

Solution

Answer: C

To avoid PMI, the primary mortgage must be not greater than 80% LTV (70% of $700,000=$490,000)

If the borrower has $70,000 to use as their down payment (which is equivalent to 10% of purchase price), a further 10% will be required to bridge the gap between his first mortgage, purchase price, and the down payment.

PRACTICE TEST THREE

1. A loan for financing the construction of a property that is eventually repaid in cash after the house is built is known as what?

A.Construction to long-term financing

B.Loan for Rehabilitation

C.Bridge loan

D.A construction loan

2. Non-conventional credit is exemplified by which of the following?

A) A car loan with fewer than ten months since it started

B) A three-month gym membership.

C) A deferred student loan.

D) An apartment that has been rented for over 1 year.

3.How long before an amended loan estimate should be issued again in the event of a severe change in circumstances??

A.So long as it is given beforeclosing, there is no exact period mandating when an amended loan estimate must be issued.

B.Within an interval of three general working days from the closing date.

C.Within an interval of three general working days from the date of valid change of circumstance.

D.Revised loan estimates are not issued because the closing disclosure objectively discloses the true cost.

4.POC stands for?

A.Paid on conversion

B.Paid outside of closing

C.Paid on condition

D.Place on contingence

5.Which of the following would be a potential solution for a buyer with few assets worth less than the outstanding debt and apprehensive about their payments?

A.Loan modification

B.Short sale

C.Deed in lieu of foreclosure

D.Just forget about it

6.When will a customer have to submit the latest two-years worth of federal tax returns?

A.They have been in their current job for less than two months

B.Buying their first home.

C.They have earned overtime bonus or commission income for less than two years

D.Their overtime bonus of the month or commission income equates to or exceeds 25% of their gross monthly base salary

7.Mary applies for a loan that exceeds the HOEPA lending limit. Along with everything else, what should her loan originator do?

A.Three working days prior to closing, provide Mary with a HOEPA-related disclosure.

B.Make a different type of financing available to her.

C.There is nothing further that needs to be done.

D.Within three working days from the day of application, send Mary a particular HOEPA-related disclosure.

8.How will the issuance of the disclosure revelation influence the debt settlement?

A.The closing would not be allowed to occur until six precise business days elapsed post-issuance.

B.There would be no required changes to the closing schedule.

C.The closing would not be allowed to occur until three precise business days occur post-issuance.

D.The closing would not be allowed to occur until seven business days occur post-issuance.

9.What is the maximum LTV possible through FHA financing?

A.94%

B.99%

C.93%

D.96.5%

10.Following the initial closing disclosure, a revised closing disclosure must be issued:

A.Once a closing disclosure is issued, no further fee changes are allowed.

B.When a regular transactions final APR exceed the final APR disclosed on the loan estimate by more than 0.25%

C.When an irregular transactions final APR exceed the APR disclosed on the loan estimate by 0.125%

D.When an irregular transaction final APR exceeds the APR disclosed on the closing disclosure by 0.25%

11. Even though he is 66 years old, a borrower requests to apply for a reverse mortgage. Joe is his 26-year-old girlfriend. What advice would an MLO give to somebody in this situation?

A.That, since his girlfriend is also an owner, he would have to remove her name from the title in order to apply for the reverse mortgage in his name.

B.No special advice as long as at least one borrower is 62 years old; they can both apply.

C.That you can take the loan application in his name only

D.That she will need to sign a consent allowing him to apply in his own name.

12.A tailor earns a salary of $2000 weekly along with a monthly untaxed social security stipend of $1050. What is his monthly income?

A.$8391.67

B.$2881.25

C.$2625.00

D.$9979.17

13.A hard copy of the following documents must be kept on the premises of all financial institutions at all times.

A.The DIDMCA

B.The FTC's guideline on identity theft detection, prevention, and mitigation.

C.The CFPB's listing of all final rules

D.The Dodd Frank Act

14.In a Judicial foreclosure:

A.A judge must order an eviction

B.Only a federal court can enforce a foreclosure

C.The mortgage does not contain a power of sale clause

D.The foreclosure is, in essence, the same as a nonjudicial foreclosure

15.Which of the following indicates potential fraud?

A.An appraisal dated before the sale contract

B.An applicant who recently changed their name

C.An employer who recently went out of business

D.A sales contract date before the appraisal

16.Prior to closing on a HOEPA loan, the borrower must

A.Be informed about their right to receive homeownership counseling along with a list of counseling agencies from their lender not later than three business days prior to closing

B.Be advised of their right to seek the advice of legal counsel

C.Secure homeownership counseling from a HUD approved counseling agency

D.Be offered a different loan that does not exceed HOEPA threshold

17.Which of the following is a repercussion of exercising one's right to rescind?

A.All the money the borrower has paid into the transaction must be paid back to them, within 20 days.

B.All of the money the borrower paid, minus the money the creditor did spent on third party settlements services, should be paid back to the borrower.

C.All money paid into the undertaking must be refunded to the borrower within 45 days of them exercising their rights to rescind

D.The applicants can't use the same lender for applications again.

18.Which of the following fees is not considered when calculating the APR?

A.The MERS fee

B.The underwriting fee

C.The credit report

D.The application fee

19.A loan originator tells a consumer who seeks to get a stated income loan how much money they need to make for the loan to work. This is unethical because:

A.Before being told, the customer did not ask the loan originator any questions.

B.A loan originator may not prompt a customer.

C.Because it is a stated loan and income is irrelevant, it is not an ethical infraction.

D.The loan originator is a participant in the deal.

20.When a mortgage loan applicant asks, "How much income do I need to qualify for a $525,000 purchase price?" what is the most ethical response?

A.If you could make $6000 each month, that would be amazing.

B.Why don't we check your pay stubs, tax returns, and asset statements to see how much money you make?

C.We evaluate 36% of your monthly earnings.

D.Everything relies on your credit score.

21. You've invited real estate agents to a presentation about your new mortgage product. You offer refreshments to the real estate agents. Is this a breach of the Reproductive Health and Safety Act of 1970 (RESPA)?

A.True

B.False

22.What is an HPML (higher-priced mortgage loan)?

A.A loan with a higher yearly percentage rate (APR) than the average prime offer rate

B.A loan with a lower yearly percentage rate (APR) than the average prime offer rate

C.A loan with a higher yearly percentage rate (APR) than a 30-year fixed loan

D.A loan having a lower yearly percentage rate than a 30-year fixed-rate loan.

23.Is a bridge loan that lasts shorter than a year exempt from the higher-cost mortgage loan?

A.True

B.False

24.You want to buy a single-family home with a higher-interest mortgage. Is this something that isn't featured on a higher-priced mortgage loan's shopping list?

A.True

B.False

25.Which of the following was passed by the United States Congress in 1974 to help customers find settlement services more easily, and to prevent kick-backs and referral fees that drive up these settlement costs?

A. TILA Act

B. RESPA Act

C. SOX Act

D.HIPAA Act

26.In the RESPA definition of a completed application, which of the following is included. Choose all that are appropriate?

A. The name of the borrower

B. Monthly income of the borrower

C. Borrowers' tax in the last two years

D. If applicable, the borrower's property data in a country other than the United States.

E.The borrower's social security number in order to obtain a credit report

F.The address of the property

G.An estimate of the property's worth

H.The Amount of the Loan

27.Can money from a reverse mortgage payment be used to pay for a wedding?

A.True

B.False

28.What does it mean to withdraw the loan?

A.In the event of home foreclosure, the borrower should auction his personal items.

B.The borrower should use his retirement funds, such as his 401k and IRA, to pay down the mortgage.

C.The borrower can cancel the loan as if it never existed

D. None of the preceding

29.You notice an advertisement for a mortgage that indicates FHA financing is available, as well as 100% Veteran loan VA financing and an easy monthly payment choice. IS THIS A VIOLATION OF THE TILA TERMS OF ADVERTISING?

A.True

B.False

30. What is the name for a loan type that provides equal monthly payments for as long as the borrower survives, while occupying the home as a primary residence?

A.A fixed-rate loan

B.A reverse mortgage is a type of loan that allows you to borrow money from Conversion Mortgage for Home Equity (HECMs)

C.Veterans Administration Loan

D. FHA (Federal Housing Administration) Loan

31.A mortgage lender recieved a lead directly from a title insurance firm. He then sends the title insurance firm a thank-you note for recommending a buyer. Is this a violation of RESPA?

A.Of course. It is the brokers mistake.

B.Yes, but it's the title insurance firm's fault for giving a gift and expecting to receive something back.

C.Both are to blame in equal measure

D.None of them are at fault because a thank-you card isn't defined as a valuable item.

32. How much is a lender's title policy worth?

A.It is equal to 50% of the loan amount

B.It is less than the loan amount

C.It is the same as the loan amount

D.None of the preceding

33.The borrower may be required to purchase title insurance by the lender. What is the reason for this?

A.After a comprehensive investigation of the title, the insurance firm issues the lender's title policy. It ensures that the title is clear and that any losses incurred as a result of title disputes will be paid. This policy's cost is the same as the loan's cost.

B.The lender can sell this coverage.

C. In the event of a home burglary, claims can be filed.

D. None of the preceding

34.Who is responsible for overseeing and supervising NMLS-member lenders, conducting background checks, and establishing rules and regulations?

A.The legislature of a state

B.The existence of a federal legislature

C.A licensing authority at the state level

D.Lawyer (attorney-at-law)

35.For one client, a title insurance firm supposes that a mortgage lender waive his earnings from the deal. In return, they say they will refer more clients in the future. Have either of then breached RESPA?

A.Both of them have

B.They aren't any of them

C.A title insurance company

D.Mortgage broker

36.What does an FHA loan's DTI mean?

A.31/43

B.31/44

C.31/44

D.32/44

37.What does DTI stand for?

A.Dual Trio information

B.Dependency Test income

C.Debt to income ratio

D.None of the preceding

38.What does URLA mean?

A.Residential Loan Application (Uniform)

B.Application for a Uniform Residential Licensing

C.A single application for a home loan

D.A single licensing authority for residential properties

39.Which credit application do you use to get a new house loan?

A.The URLA (Uniform Residential Loan Application)

B.Form 1003 of the FNMA

C.Form 65 of the FHLMC

D.They're all the same

E.None of the above

40.What are the six main components that make up a live application?

A.Social Security number

B.The value of the assets

C.Monthly earnings

D.Property value estimate

E.Your birth date

F.The location of the property

G.The Amount of the Loan

41. What is the definition of the term "cost of credit" in terms of interest rate?

A.The ARM

B.The APR

C.A flat rate

D.A float rate is a rate that fluctuates from one day to the next.

42.Is the annual percentage rate (APR) the rate that is used to compute monthly payment of a loan?

A.Yes, it is always true

B.Annual Percentage Rate (APR) refers to the cost of acquiring a loan, which is defined as the interest rate.

C. Of course. It is the expense of determining the loan repayment amount.

D.It is subject to change.

43.What is the need for financial institutions to provide to all clients under the Gramm-Leach-Billy Act at the time of establishing a client relationship??

A.A copy of the Privacy Statement for the Company

B.A copy of APR

C. The final loan repayment calculations

D.A certified copy of the evaluation value

44. In accordance with the Gramm-Leach-Bliley Act, when is a client relationship with a financial institution accepted and a privacy notice delivered to the customer?

A.At the beginning, while a buyer is applying for a loan.

B.When a client chooses to lock in an interest rate.

C.When a client completes the house's construction.

D.At the conclusion of the transaction

45.A financial institution is required under the Gramm-Leach-Bliley Act to issue each customer with a copy of its privacy notice at the time of closing, also known as customer related time. Is it necessary to give consumers privacy warnings? If that's the case, how often do you do it?

A.There is no need to supply anything after this.

B.Yes, this must be done on a three-month basis after that.

C.Yes, this must be done every six months after that.

D.Yes, this must be done every year after that.

46.Is it true that the Gramm-Leach-Bliley Act only requires financial institutions to give privacy notices to their consumers once a year in paper form?

A.Yes, this must be sent solely on paper.

B.No way, this has to be done just online.

C.No, In some situations, this can be sent in print format as well as posted online.

D.None of the preceding

47.Which form of reverse mortgage loan converts a senior's home equity into cash?

A.A set rate

B.A float rate is a rate that fluctuates from one day to the next.

C.The ARM

D.HECM

Answer : D

Explanation: A home equity conversion mortgage, as the name implies, allows senior homeowners to convert their home equity into capital.. This is a reverse mortgage application.

48. When is it necessary for a lender to renew a mortgage license?

A.Two years period

B.Three years period

C.One calendar year period

D.Six months

49. What is the duration of a Mortgage Loan Organizer license?

A.The 30th of November

B.The 31st of December

C.The 31st of August

D.The 31st of October

50.When does a credit card with interest become a problem?

A. When the final payment deadline is the first day of the month after the closure date.

B.When the first payment is due on the last day of the month, right after the bank closes.

C.When the final payment deadline is the 15th of the month after the closure date.

D.Regardless of the payment deadline, immediately after the closing.

51.Answer: Someone who wants to steal people's identities distributes a form among the community's residents. What actions will be brought against this person if he is captured?

A.Postal Fraud

B.Theft of a credit card

C.Money Laundering

D.Laundering of mail

52.The prospective client is not submitting an application to the USDA, the State Bond Program, or Community Lending. Is it mandatory for them to reveal their incomes?

A.No, this is purely voluntary.

B.Of course. It is required.

C.In the case of USDA loans, income disclosure is required.

D.Any form of loan requires income disclosure.

53.What is the objective of any financial institution's CIP?

A.Customers must be identified and verified to be who they say they are.

B.To assist clients who have lost their jobs, offer low-interest loans based on their credit scores.

C.To assist customers who have lost their jobs.

D.Verify that the appraisal was completed appropriately.

54.Is it legal under RESPA to trade anything valuable between existing or potential referral sources?

A.Of course. According to RESPA, it is permissible.

B.Yes. each time a transaction is made, it should be reported to NMLS.

C.Yes, according to RESPA, nothing of value should be exchanged.

D.There are several exceptions, such as gift cards, which are not allowed..

55.On a traditional loan, when is private mortgage insurance (PMI) required?

A.When a buyer has less than a 25% down payment for a home or when a customer refinances a loan with a loan-to-value (LTV) of more than 80%.

B. When a buyer has less than 30% equity in a home or when a customer refinances a loan with a loan-to-value (LTV) of more than 80%.

C.When a buyer has less than 20% equity in a home or when a customer refinances a loan with a loan-to-value (LTV) of greater than 70%.

D.When the buyer has less than 20% equity in the home or when the client refinances with a loan-to-value (LTV) of more than 80%.

56.While creating loan application documents, why is it important for a lender to think about it?

A.To repay their loan, the applicant must have a good credit history.

B.The borrower's parents are wealthy, therefore in the event of default, the loan can be easily repaid.

C.The applicant's ability to repay the loan is easily determined by their income in relation to their present expenses.

D.Borrowers have a certain number of years to repay the loan

57. Under the Fair Credit Reporting Act, what are Creditor-like bodies that provide credit-related details about loan consumers to a credit reporting agency (CRA) called?

A.Furnishers

B.Creditors

C.Amortgagor

D.Keep an eye on things.

58. What should a refinance provider do if a primary mortgage is repaid but a secondary loan is kept?

A.Agree to be subordinated

B.Sign the Decree of Consent

C.Acknowledge collateral

D.Execute a promissory note

59.When a policy is enacted, it inadvertently and negatively impacts a specific set of individuals. What is this policy's name?

A.The influence of affinity

B.Inequitable impact

C.How does fraud affect policy?

D.The impact of race

60.A mortgage firm chooses to inform its consumers about a new process. They have chosen to use only email for correspondence. Is this a disproportionate effect?

A -No, email is the preferred method of communication, and all customers are required to have email-capable devices.

B - During registration, clients would have chosen their preffered correspondence type, so there is no disproportionate effect.

C - This is unimportant because this is merely a message.

D - Yes, there is a disproportionate impact because it affects customers who do not use electronic devices to read emails due to financial constraints.

61.At what time is a fresh final concluding disclosure available?

A.When the final charges of the loan exceed the final disclosure finance charge by more than $ 1000.

B.The final disclosure is derived from the financing charge when the total financial charge on the loan surpasses $10,000.

C.The final disclosure is from the finance charge when the loan's ultimate finance charge exceeds $100,000.

D.When the loan's final finance charge exceeds the final disclosure finance charge by more than $100.

Answer: D

62.In which circumstances will the NMLS-approved course be accepted for credit

A.Regardless of the conditions

B.When the training satisfies federal legal and ethical requirements.

C.When the course is approved for a non-traditional mortgage.

D. When the program complies with federal regulations, non-traditional mortgages, and ethical guidelines.

63.Which of the following factors makes it impossible for a mortgage lender to grant a negative waiver?

A.APY (Annual Percentage Yield) Payment Cap

a.Payment cap for ARMs

b.A payment term of 30 years

c.A payment term of 15 years

64.In regard to BSA/AML, What does CIP stand for?

A.Customer Index Program

B.Customer Identification Program

C.Calculated Identification Program

65.A client is requesting a loan that is not part of the USDA, community loan, or state bond programs. They do, however, choose to declare their earnings of their own volition. What is the next step? Make a list of everything that is appropriate.

A. Earnings are able to be declared as they are.

B.A court must issue an order for the income.

C.There is no requirement for a receipt.

D.A receipt history is established

E.It is necessary to demonstrate continuity.

66.The State Licensing Body issues licenses to individuals. They later discovered that the man had committed arson, which would have automatically disqualified him. What should the state licensing authority do in this case?

A. The license can be revoked at any time, but the individual can still conduct business.

B.It could prevent a licensed individual from doing any more business until a final decision is made.

C. Allows a person to conduct business under certain restrictions.

D.The body is powerless because the license has already been granted.

67.The ECOA was passed by Congress in 1974 for what reason?

A.To ensure that applicants for credit are not unfairly treated.

B.Examine credit applicants' federal tax returns.

C.To avoid the risks of non-mortgage items

D.To to do away with the PMI that is brought with VA loans.

68.What are the advantages of fraud and active duty alerts to clients? Choose everything that is appropriate.

A.There is no protection

B.If they have previously been a victim of fraud, they will be given additional protection.

C.If they are in the military, they will have additional security.

D.If they are deployed, they will provide additional protection.

69.What should the debt initiator issue to the applicant within three business days of the date of application, among other things?

A.Credit report

B.Loan Estimate

C.Evaluation

D.Property Title Insurance

70. What is the name of a policy that harms a specific group of people inadvertently?

A.The Direct Effect

B.Inequitable Impact

C.Indirect Influence

D.Total Effect

71.A prospective buyer desires to fund their own investment with a down payment of 15%. What percentage of the purchase price can a seller deduct as a seller's discount?

A.1%

B.9%

C.6%

D.2%

72.USDA loan allows a maximum of what loan-to-value ratio?

A.0%

B.100%

C.20%

D.15%

73.What has helped to lower the number of incidences of fraud involving third-party foreclosure negotiators?

A.Negotiators can collect a fee for showing the foreclosed property

B.Negotiators may collect a fee once a successful negotiation has occurred.

C.Increased negotiator expenses may occur from pre-negotiations.

D.None of the preceding.

74.All and any Outstanding liens and encumbrances can be found on which page of the title insurance binder?

A.A Schedule

B.B Schedule

C.C Schedule

D.D Schedule

75. Is this a personal loan or a business loan if everything in the loan file that is being delivered to a loan originator for financing is incorrect, fabricated, and deceitful?

A.A fixed-rate loan

B.Loan that floats

C.Loan obtained by deception

D.Air Loans

76.Is it a red flag when comparables that are far away from the subject property are used when a rural property is appraised?

A.Yes, the appraisal should include comparables within a 20-mile radius.

B.Yes, comparable properties within a 3-mile radius must be utilized in the appraisal.

C.No, It is not necessary for the appraisal to be a red flag, and it can be approved - as there are no similar properties in the vicinity.

D. None of the preceding

77.What do you call fraud concerns in the mortgage process?

A.Red flags

B.Blue Flags

C.Flags of yellow

D.Flags of white

78.You get a loan request for $484500 on a single-family home, which is more than the traditional mortgage maximum. Which loan will you use to finance this purchase?

A.Jumbo Financing

B.ARM (Alternative Refinancing Mortgage)

C.FHA-insured mortgages

79.A VA loan application is sent to you. Because the property purchase price exceeds $489000, you must determine whether a 0% downpayment is appropriate for this loan application. What decision will you make as a loan originator?

A.0%

B.25%

C.15%

D.5%

80.Which constitutional statute prevents fraudulently claiming through advertising and promotion that the government has sponsored a particular program, item, or service?

A.RESPA (Reform of the Civil Service Act)

B.TILA (Title Insurance and Liability Act)

C.ECOA is a non-profit organization that promotes environmental awareness.

D.GIBA

81.Which legislation is primarily concerned with identifying and combating workplace discrimination?

A.ECOA (Environmental Conservation Agency of the United States) RESPA (Reform of the Civil Service Act)

B. RESPA (Reform of the Civil Service Act)

C.TILA (Title Insurance and Liability Act)

D. HMDA (Health and Medical Devices Act)

82.A borrower makes a $500,000 purchase. They put down a 25% deposit. The borrower selects an interest rate that is higher than the market rate and receives a 1% closing cost credit. In this circumstance, what is the maximum amount to which settlement costs can be reduced?

A. $2250

B.$3000

C.$2800

D.$3100

83.What is the housing expense ratio of a client with an annual income of $100,000 and housing expenses of $2100?

A.25.2%

B.35.2%

C.30%

D.24%

84.Can a borrower excessively force a lender to refinance solely for his personal benefit without providing the borrower with a real net tangible benefit?

A.Yes, this is permissible.

B.No, a refinance must always provide a net tangible advantage to the borrower.

C.This is authorized for fixed-rate loans.

D.This is permitted in the case of ARM

85.A Commissioner has some reservations regarding a licensee's formal request for justification. What else could he possibly want?

A.Licensee's books and records

B.Licensee's book

C.Licensee's records

D.None of the above

86.What kind of insurance does the guarantor provide to the lender in the event that the lender causes harm to someone?

A.They may submit a claim for compensation for Carelessness, inability, or delinquency.

B.Mistreated, ineptitude, and wrongdoing may result in a claim that can be easily dismissed.

C.Carelessness, ineptitude, and wrongdoing can result in bodily injury to a person.

D.All of the above

87.What happens to the lender if a warranty bond claim is ever paid?

A.They are not permitted to originate until a compensation assurance is acquired.

B.They will be unable to obtain loans for the rest of their lives.

C.They are not allowed to take out a loan for a year.

D.They are qualified to work as a real estate agent

88.How long does it take to remove an MIP?

A.After 9 years

B.After 10 years

C.After 11 years

D.After a period of 12 years

89.What is the most significant benefit of some lenders' capacity to float down?

A.If tariffs fall before the deadline, the borrower can request a one-time tariff reduction.

B.If tariffs fall before the deadline, the borrower can apply for a one-time tariff reduction.

C.Borrower can make plea for a triple of the amount if prices fall after closing.

D.If prices fall after closing, the applicant can request a tripling of the price.

90.After locking in their interest rates, some lenders offer a float-down option to their clients. If the interest rate lowers before the closing date, this allows for a one-time interest rate reduction. What is gathered from customers in exchange for this benefit?

A.This is a complimentary benefit.

B.This is a benefit that comes with an additional point fee at the conclusion of the transaction.

C.Clients are allowed to pay what they choose.

D.Clients must provide a monetary deposit.

91. The loan originator is currently working on a loan for a client who has recently moved employment. Is this behavior a cause for concern?

A.Without a doubt. Change of employment while processing a loan is a red flag.

B.No, this is not a red flag.

C.This is a red flag.

D.This is a case where the white flag should be raised.

PRACTICE TEST THREE - ANSWERS

1.A loan for financing the construction of a property that is eventually repaid in cash after the house is built is known as what?

A.Construction to long-term financing

B.Loan for Rehabilitation

C.Bridge loan

D.A construction loan

Answer: D, Construction loans fund the building of a home on unusually undeveloped land and are repaid once the project is finished. Construction on perpetual loans become 'Final Loans' once the build is completed. A rehabilitation loan is used to fund the rehabilitation and repair of an existing home, whereas a bridge loan is used for short-term financing.

2.Non-conventional credit is exemplified by which of the following?

A) A car loan with fewer than ten months since it started

B) A three-month gym membership.

C) A deferred student loan.

D) An apartment that has been rented for over 1 year.

Answer, D: Non-traditional credit is credit that does not appear on a consumer's credit report. When the applicant has lacking/no credit history, a guarantor may use a non-conventional credit report to obtain certain types of loans. At least four trading lines, one of which must be residential, must be included in an unconventional credit report. All trade lines used must have a minimum of a twelve-month history, hence D is the correct answer.

3.How long before an amended loan estimate should be issued again in the event of a severe change in circumstances??

A.So long as it is given beforeclosing, there is no exact period mandating when an amended loan estimate must be issued.

B.Within an interval of three general working days from the closing date.

C.Within an interval of three general working days from the date of valid change of circumstance.

D.Revised loan estimates are not issued because the closing disclosure objectively discloses the true cost.

Answer: C, In the case of a correct change of circumstances, an amended loan estimate shall be given within three regular working days from the date of change of circumstances.

4.POC stands for?

A.Paid on conversion

B.Paid outside of closing

C.Paid on condition

D.Place on contingence

Answer: B

If a borrower pays for any settlement fee or any other cost before closing, the cost is instead listed on the loan estimate as paid outside of closing.

5.Which of the following would be a potential solution for a buyer with few assets worth less than the outstanding debt and apprehensive about their payments?

A.Loan modification

B.Short sale

C.Deed in lieu of foreclosure

D.Just forget about it

Answer: A

If the borrower has minimal assets, he would not be able to sell the home unless his lender allows a short sale. A short sale may also result in a deficiency judgment - for the difference between the loan balance and the amount for which the lender released the lien. The third option, A deed in lieu of foreclosure would crucially damage his credit, so this is no good. Ignoring the problem would not alleviate it. Therefore, a modification to more manageable loan terms would likely be the best solution.

6.When will a customer have to submit the latest two-years worth of federal tax returns?

A.They have been in their current job for less than two months

B.Buying their first home.

C.They have earned overtime bonus or commission income for less than two years

D.Their overtime bonus of the month or commission income equates to or exceeds 25% of their gross monthly base salary

Answer: D

When using bonus for overtime or commission earnings to qualify for mortgage financing, standard investor procedure requires applicants to present their most recent two-year federal tax returns. This should be done whenever the monthly income is equal to or exceeds 25% of their base, total monthly income. This demonstrates consistent earning of income as well as it's likelihood to continue.

7.Mary applies for a loan that exceeds the HOEPA lending limit. Along with everything else, what should her loan originator do?

A.Three working days prior to closing, provide Mary with a HOEPA-related disclosure.

B.Make a different type of financing available to her.

C.There is nothing further that needs to be done.

D.Within three working days from the day of application, send Mary a particular HOEPA-related disclosure.

Answer: A

Anyone who defaults on a loan that exceeds the terms that classify the loan as a HOEPA loan must get a specific HOEPA disclosure that does not exceed three working days before closing. Should: Informs them that the loan will not work until completion or when their account is opened, defines default results, exposes loan parameters such as APR, monthly payments Specifies the amount borrowed, and if the loan is ARM, and the maximum monthly HOEPA payment.

8.How will the issuance of the disclosure revelation influence the debt settlement?

A.The closing would not be allowed to occur until six precise business days elapsed post-issuance.

B.There would be no required changes to the closing schedule.

C.The closing would not be allowed to occur until three precise business days occur post-issuance.

D.The closing would not be allowed to occur until seven business days occur post-issuance.

Answer: C

When an amended closing disclosure is issued, three more business days must elapse before the customer completes the transaction to give the user ample time to evaluate the changes they have made.

9.What is the maximum LTV possible through FHA financing?

A.94%

B.99%

C.93%

D.96.5%

Answer: D

The minimum payment under FHA is 3.5 percent. As a result, the greatest LTV achievable through a minimum down payment is 96.5 percent.

10.Following the initial closing disclosure, a revised closing disclosure must be issued:

A.Once a closing disclosure is issued, no further fee changes are allowed.

B.When a regular transactions final APR exceed the final APR disclosed on the loan estimate by more than 0.25%

C.When an irregular transactions final APR exceed the APR disclosed on the loan estimate by 0.125%

D.When an irregular transaction final APR exceeds the APR disclosed on the closing disclosure by 0.25%

Answer: D

Once the closing disclosure has been issued, a revised closing disclosure disclosing specific causes must be issued when the loan's final APR deviates from the APR disclosed on the closing disclosure by more than 0.125% for a regular transaction or by 0.25% for an irregular transaction, the loan changes or a prepayment penalty is added into the loan.

11. Even though he is 66 years old, a borrower requests to apply for a reverse mortgage. Joe is his 26-year-old girlfriend. What advice would an MLO give to somebody in this situation?

A.That, since his girlfriend is also an owner, he would have to remove her name from the title in order to apply for the reverse mortgage in his name.

B.No special advice as long as at least one borrower is 62 years old; they can both apply.

C.That you can take the loan application in his name only

D.That she will need to sign a consent allowing him to apply in his own name.

Answer: A

Because a reverse mortgage is an FHA loan, no one should be mortgaged on the home's title. The only exception to the reverse mortgage is if the borrower's spouse is under the age of 62; his girlfriend is under the age of 62 and has no spouse, so she is not eligible for a reverse mortgage. He must relinquish his ownership interest in the house to apply in his name because he is also on the title. However, if she was his wife, she could keep the title if he took out a reverse mortgage in her name and paid it off. This should not be done without first consulting with a qualified legal and/or income tax professional.

12.A tailor earns a salary of $2000 weekly along with a monthly untaxed social security stipend of $1050. What is his monthly income?

A.$8391.67

B.$2881.25

C.$2625.00

D.$9979.17

Answer: D

Annual income = 2000*52 = $104,000

His annual income of $104,000 translates to a monthly income of

104000/12 = $8666.67

Since his monthly social security income is untaxed, this can be increased by 25%

25% of 1050 = $262.5

262.5+1050 =$1312.5

Which, when added to the monthly salary of $8666.67, results in a monthly income of $9979.17

13.A hard copy of the following documents must be kept on the premises of all financial institutions at all times.

A.The DIDMCA

B.The FTC's guideline on identity theft detection, prevention, and mitigation.

C.The CFPB's listing of all final rules

D.The Dodd Frank Act

Answer: B

Because, If the FTC requested a copy of the guidelines during an audit and they didn't show one, the financial organisation could be fined.

14.In a Judicial foreclosure:

A.A judge must order an eviction

B.Only a federal court can enforce a foreclosure

C.The mortgage does not contain a power of sale clause

D.The foreclosure is, in essence, the same as a nonjudicial foreclosure

Answer: C

If a mortgage does not have a power of sale clause, the lender must take the route of judicial foreclosure.

15.Which of the following indicates potential fraud?

A.An appraisal dated before the sale contract

B.An applicant who recently changed their name

C.An employer who recently went out of business

D.A sales contract date before the appraisal

Answer: A

Appraisals should always be dated after the sales contract.

16.Prior to closing on a HOEPA loan, the borrower must

A.Be informed about their right to receive homeownership counseling along with a list of counseling agencies from their lender not later than three business days prior to closing

B.Be advised of their right to seek the advice of legal counsel

C.Secure homeownership counseling from a HUD approved counseling agency

D.Be offered a different loan that does not exceed HOEPA threshold

Answer: C

17.Which of the following is a repercussion of exercising one's right to rescind?

A.All the money the borrower has paid into the transaction must be paid back to them, within 20 days.

B.All of the money the borrower paid, minus the money the creditor did spent on third party settlements services, should be paid back to the borrower.

C.All money paid into the undertaking must be refunded to the borrower within 45 days of them exercising their rights to rescind

D.The applicants can't use the same lender for applications again.

Solution: A

18.Which of the following fees is not considered when calculating the APR?

A.The MERS fee

B.The underwriting fee

C.The credit report

D.The application fee

Answer: D

19.A loan originator tells a consumer who seeks to get a stated income loan how much money they need to make for the loan to work. This is unethical because:

A.Before being told, the customer did not ask the loan originator any questions.

B.A loan originator may not prompt a customer.

C.Because it is a stated loan and income is irrelevant, it is not an ethical infraction.

D.The loan originator is a participant in the deal.

Answer: B

The customer must declare their income under a stated loan scheme. Despite the fact that income is not always verified, stated income frequently leads to DTIs that must be kept below allowed levels. A loan originator should never compel a customer to say what is required rather than what is right.

20.When a mortgage loan applicant asks, "How much income do I need to qualify for a $525,000 purchase price?" what is the most ethical response?

A.If you could make $6000 each month, that would be amazing.

B.Why don't we check your pay stubs, tax returns, and asset statements to see how much money you make?

C.We evaluate 36% of your monthly earnings.

D.Everything relies on your credit score.

Answer: B

A loan originator should never attempt to persuade a customer to submit a better loan application. The loan originator should simply examine the customer's qualifications and make recommendations based on them.

21. You've invited real estate agents to a presentation about your new mortgage product. You offer refreshments to the real estate agents. Is this a breach of the Reproductive Health and Safety Act of 1970 (RESPA)?

A.True

B.False

Answer: A, True

Reasoning: Under RESPA, educational exchanges such as webinars (or) seminars, as well as the sharing of appropriate promotional items like fliers promoting new products, are permissible. The refreshment is a valuable object that should not be sold or transferred between mortgage brokers and realtors since it falls outside the agreement's boundaries. Because realtors are potential referral sources, this is a breach of RESPA (Real Estate Settlement Procedures Act).

22.What is an HPML (higher-priced mortgage loan)?

A.A loan with a higher yearly percentage rate (APR) than the average prime offer rate

B.A loan with a lower yearly percentage rate (APR) than the average prime offer rate

C.A loan with a higher yearly percentage rate (APR) than a 30-year fixed loan

D.A loan having a lower yearly percentage rate than a 30-year fixed-rate loan.

Answer: A

23.Is a bridge loan that lasts shorter than a year exempt from the higher-cost mortgage loan?

A.True

B.False

Answer: A, True

Explanation: All HPML loan limits are waived for bridge loans of 12 months or less used to purchase a principal residence.

24.You want to buy a single-family home with a higher-interest mortgage. Is this something that isn't featured on a higher-priced mortgage loan's shopping list?

A.True

B.False

Answer: B, False

Explanation: Construction loans for the initial construction of a home, bridging loans with loan terms of 12 months or less, reverse mortgages, HELOCs, qualifying mortgages as defined in Regulation Z, new manufactured home loans, loans secured by mobile homes, yachts, and automobiles are all exemptions.

25.Which of the following was passed by the United States Congress in 1974 to help customers find settlement services more easily, and to prevent kickbacks and referral fees that drive up these settlement costs?

A. TILA Act

B. RESPA Act

C. SOX Act

D.HIPAA Act

Answer: B

Explanation: The Real Estate Settlement Procedures Act meets this requirement and makes it easier for people to buy a house. This keeps the settlement service provider honest by eliminating indirect referral transactions like things of value transacted between mortgage lenders and potential referral sources like realtors.

26.In the RESPA definition of a completed application, which of the following is included. Choose all that are appropriate?

A. The name of the borrower

B. Monthly income of the borrower

C. Borrowers' tax in the last two years

D. If applicable, the borrower's property data in a country other than the United States.

E.The borrower's social security number in order to obtain a credit report

F.The address of the property

G.An estimate of the property's worth

H.The Amount of the Loan

Correct answers

: A B E F G H

27.Can money from a reverse mortgage payment be used to pay for a wedding?

A.True

B.False

Answer: A, True

Explanation: The funds from a reverse mortgage can be used for any purpose.

28.What does it mean to withdraw the loan?

A.In the event of home foreclosure, the borrower should auction his personal items.

B.The borrower should use his retirement funds, such as his 401k and IRA, to pay down the mortgage.

C.The borrower can cancel the loan as if it never existed

D. None of the preceding

Answer: C

29.You notice an advertisement for a mortgage that indicates FHA financing is available, as well as 100% Veteran loan VA financing and an easy monthly payment choice. IS THIS A VIOLATION OF THE TILA TERMS OF ADVERTISING?

A.True

B.False

Answer: B, False

30. What is the name for a loan type that provides equal monthly payments for as long as the borrower survives, while occupying the home as a primary residence?

A.A fixed-rate loan

B.A reverse mortgage is a type of loan that allows you to borrow money from Conversion Mortgage for Home Equity (HECMs)

C.Veterans Administration Loan

D. FHA (Federal Housing Administration) Loan

Answer: B

31.A mortgage lender recieved a lead directly from a title insurance firm. He then sends the title insurance firm a thank-you note for recommending a buyer. Is this a violation of RESPA?

A.Of course. It is the brokers mistake.

B.Yes, but it's the title insurance firm's fault for giving a gift and expecting to receive something back.

C.Both are to blame in equal measure

D.None of them are at fault because a thank-you card isn't defined as a valuable item.

Answer: D

32. How much is a lender's title policy worth?

A.It is equal to 50% of the loan amount

B.It is less than the loan amount

C.It is the same as the loan amount

D.None of the preceding

Answer: C

33.The borrower may be required to purchase title insurance by the lender. What is the reason for this?

A.After a comprehensive investigation of the title, the insurance firm issues the lender's title policy. It ensures that the title is clear and that any losses incurred as a result of title disputes will be paid. This policy's cost is the same as the loan's cost.

B.The lender can sell this coverage.

C. In the event of a home burglary, claims can be filed.

D. None of the preceding

Answer: A

34.Who is responsible for overseeing and supervising NMLS-member lenders, conducting background checks, and establishing rules and regulations?

A.The legislature of a state

B.The existence of a federal legislature

C.A licensing authority at the state level

D.Lawyer (attorney-at-law)

Answer: C

35.For one client, a title insurance firm supposes that a mortgage lender waive his earnings from the deal. In return, they say they will refer more clients in the future. Have either of then breached RESPA?

A.Both of them have

B.They aren't any of them

C.A title insurance company

D.Mortgage broker

Answer: A

Explanation: When one of them contributes something worthwhile, according to RESPA, value is created. This is a crime.

36.What does an FHA loan's DTI mean?

A.31/43

B.31/44

C.31/44

D.32/44

Answer: A

Explanation: An FHA loan allows you to receive a loan with a high DTI (debt-to-income ratio) while considering other aspects such as down payment, credit score, and so on.

37.What does DTI stand for?

A.Dual Trio information

B.Dependency Test income

C.Debt to income ratio

D.None of the preceding

Answer: C

38.What does URLA mean?

A.Residential Loan Application (Uniform)

B.Application for a Uniform Residential Licensing

C.A single application for a home loan

D.A single licensing authority for residential properties

Answer: A

39.Which credit application do you use to get a new house loan?

A.The URLA (Uniform Residential Loan Application)

B.Form 1003 of the FNMA

C.Form 65 of the FHLMC

D.They're all the same

E.None of the above

Answer : D

40.What are the six main components that make up a live application?

A.Social Security number

B.The value of the assets

C.Monthly earnings

D.Property value estimate

E.Your birth date

F.The location of the property

G.The Amount of the Loan

Answer : a,c,d,f,g,h

Explanation: A direct application requires six items: a Social Security number, a loan amount, a property valuation, a property address, a date of birth, and a monthly income.

41. What is the definition of the term "cost of credit" in terms of interest rate?

A.The ARM

B.The APR

C.A flat rate

D.A float rate is a rate that fluctuates from one day to the next.

Answer: B

42.Is the annual percentage rate (APR) the rate that is used to compute monthly payment of a loan?

A.Yes, it is always true

B.Annual Percentage Rate (APR) refers to the cost of acquiring a loan, which is defined as the interest rate.

C. Of course. It is the expense of determining the loan repayment amount.

D.It is subject to change.

Answer: B

43.What is the need for financial institutions to provide to all clients under the Gramm-Leach-Billy Act at the time of establishing a client relationship??

A.A copy of the Privacy Statement for the Company

B.A copy of APR

C. The final loan repayment calculations

D.A certified copy of the evaluation value

Answer: A

44. In accordance with the Gramm-Leach-Bliley Act, when is a client relationship with a financial institution accepted and a privacy notice delivered to the customer?

A.At the beginning, while a buyer is applying for a loan.

B.When a client chooses to lock in an interest rate.

C.When a client completes the house's construction.

D.At the conclusion of the transaction

Answer : D

45.A financial institution is required under the Gramm-Leach-Bliley Act to issue each customer with a copy of its privacy notice at the time of closing, also known as customer related time. Is it necessary to give consumers privacy warnings? If that's the case, how often do you do it?

A.There is no need to supply anything after this.

B.Yes, this must be done on a three-month basis after that.

C.Yes, this must be done every six months after that.

D.Yes, this must be done every year after that.

Answer : D

46.Is it true that the Gramm-Leach-Bliley Act only requires financial institutions to give privacy notices to their consumers once a year in paper form?

A.Yes, this must be sent solely on paper.

B.No way, this has to be done just online.

C.No, In some situations, this can be sent in print format as well as posted online.

D.None of the preceding

Answer: C

47.Which form of reverse mortgage loan converts a senior's home equity into cash?

A.A set rate

B.A float rate is a rate that fluctuates from one day to the next.

C.The ARM

D.HECM

Answer : D

Explanation: A home equity conversion mortgage, as the name implies, allows senior homeowners to convert their home equity into capital.. This is a reverse mortgage application.

48. When is it necessary for a lender to renew a mortgage license?

A.Two years period

B.Three years period

C.One calendar year period

D.Six months

Answer: C

49. What is the duration of a Mortgage Loan Organizer license?

A.The 30th of November

B.The 31st of December

C.The 31st of August

D.The 31st of October

Answer: B

50.When does a credit card with interest become a problem?

A. When the final payment deadline is the first day of the month after the closure date.

B.When the first payment is due on the last day of the month, right after the bank closes.

C.When the final payment deadline is the 15th of the month after the closure date.

D.Regardless of the payment deadline, immediately after the closing.

Answer: A

51.Answer: Someone who wants to steal people's identities distributes a form among the community's residents. What actions will be brought against this person if he is captured?

A.Postal Fraud

B.Theft of a credit card

C.Money Laundering

D.Laundering of mail

Answer: A

52.The prospective client is not submitting an application to the USDA, the State Bond Program, or Community Lending. Is it mandatory for them to reveal their incomes?

A.No, this is purely voluntary.

B.Of course. It is required.

C.In the case of USDA loans, income disclosure is required.

D.Any form of loan requires income disclosure.

Answer: A

53.What is the objective of any financial institution's CIP?

A.Customers must be identified and verified to be who they say they are.

B.To assist clients who have lost their jobs, offer low-interest loans based on their credit scores.

C.To assist customers who have lost their jobs.

D.Verify that the appraisal was completed appropriately.

Answer: A

54.Is it legal under RESPA to trade anything valuable between existing or potential referral sources?

A.Of course. According to RESPA, it is permissible.

B.Yes. each time a transaction is made, it should be reported to NMLS.

C.Yes, according to RESPA, nothing of value should be exchanged.

D.There are several exceptions, such as gift cards, which are not allowed..

Answer: C

55.On a traditional loan, when is private mortgage insurance (PMI) required?

A.When a buyer has less than a 25% down payment for a home or when a customer refinances a loan with a loan-to-value (LTV) of more than 80%.

B. When a buyer has less than 30% equity in a home or when a customer refinances a loan with a loan-to-value (LTV) of more than 80%.

C.When a buyer has less than 20% equity in a home or when a customer refinances a loan with a loan-to-value (LTV) of greater than 70%.

D.When the buyer has less than 20% equity in the home or when the client refinances with a loan-to-value (LTV) of more than 80%.

Answer: D

56.While creating loan application documents, why is it important for a lender to think about it?

A.To repay their loan, the applicant must have a good credit history.

B.The borrower's parents are wealthy, therefore in the event of default, the loan can be easily repaid.

C.The applicant's ability to repay the loan is easily determined by their income in relation to their present expenses.

D.Borrowers have a certain number of years to repay the loan

Answer: C

57. Under the Fair Credit Reporting Act, what are Creditor-like bodies that provide credit-related details about loan consumers to a credit reporting agency (CRA) called?

A.Furnishers

B.Creditors

C.Amortgagor

D.Keep an eye on things.

Answer: A

58. What should a refinance provider do if a primary mortgage is repaid but a secondary loan is kept?

A.Agree to be subordinated

B.Sign the Decree of Consent

C.Acknowledge collateral

D.Execute a promissory note

Answer: A

59.When a policy is enacted, it inadvertently and negatively impacts a specific set of individuals. What is this policy's name?

A.The influence of affinity

B.Inequitable impact

C.How does fraud affect policy?

D.The impact of race

Answer: B

60.A mortgage firm chooses to inform its consumers about a new process. They have chosen to use only email for correspondence. Is this a disproportionate effect?

A -No, email is the preferred method of communication, and all customers are required to have email-capable devices.

B - During registration, clients would have chosen their preffered correspondence type, so there is no disproportionate effect.

C - This is unimportant because this is merely a message.

D - Yes, there is a disproportionate impact because it affects customers who do not use electronic devices to read emails due to financial constraints.

Answer: D

61.At what time is a fresh final concluding disclosure available?

A.When the final charges of the loan exceed the final disclosure finance charge by more than $ 1000.

B.The final disclosure is derived from the financing charge when the total financial charge on the loan surpasses $10,000.

C.The final disclosure is from the finance charge when the loan's ultimate finance charge exceeds $100,000.

D.When the loan's final finance charge exceeds the final disclosure finance charge by more than $100.

Answer: D

62.In which circumstances will the NMLS-approved course be accepted for credit

A.Regardless of the conditions

B.When the training satisfies federal legal and ethical requirements.

C.When the course is approved for a non-traditional mortgage.

D. When the program complies with federal regulations, non-traditional mortgages, and ethical guidelines.

Answer: C

63.Which of the following factors makes it impossible for a mortgage lender to grant a negative waiver?

A.APY (Annual Percentage Yield) Payment Cap

a.Payment cap for ARMs

b.A payment term of 30 years

c.A payment term of 15 years

Answer: B

64.In regard to BSA/AML, What does CIP stand for?

A.Customer Index Program

B.Customer Identification Program

C.Calculated Identification Program

Answer: B

65.A client is requesting a loan that is not part of the USDA, community loan, or state bond programs. They do, however, choose to declare their earnings of their own volition. What is the next step? Make a list of everything that is appropriate.

A. Earnings are able to be declared as they are.

B.A court must issue an order for the income.

C.There is no requirement for a receipt.

D.A receipt history is established

E.It is necessary to demonstrate continuity.

Answer: B,D,E

66.The State Licensing Body issues licenses to individuals. They later discovered that the man had committed arson, which would have automatically disqualified him. What should the state licensing authority do in this case?

A. The license can be revoked at any time, but the individual can still conduct business.

B.It could prevent a licensed individual from doing any more business until a final decision is made.

C. Allows a person to conduct business under certain restrictions.

D.The body is powerless because the license has already been granted.

Answer: B

67.The ECOA was passed by Congress in 1974 for what reason?

A.To ensure that applicants for credit are not unfairly treated.

B.Examine credit applicants' federal tax returns.

C.To avoid the risks of non-mortgage items

D.To to do away with the PMI that is brought with VA loans.

Answer: A

68.What are the advantages of fraud and active duty alerts to clients? Choose everything that is appropriate.

A.There is no protection

B.If they have previously been a victim of fraud, they will be given additional protection.

C.If they are in the military, they will have additional security.

D.If they are deployed, they will provide additional protection.

Answer: B,C,D

69.What should the debt initiator issue to the applicant within three business days of the date of application, among other things?

A.Credit report

B.Loan Estimate

C.Evaluation

D.Property Title Insurance

Answer: B

70. What is the name of a policy that harms a specific group of people inadvertently?

A.The Direct Effect

B.Inequitable Impact

C.Indirect Influence

D.Total Effect

Answer: B

71.A prospective buyer desires to fund their own investment with a down payment of 15%. What percentage of the purchase price can a seller deduct as a seller's discount?

A.1%

B.9%

C.6%

D.2%

Answer: C

72.USDA loan allows a maximum of what loan-to-value ratio?

A.0%

B.100%

C.20%

D.15%

Answer: B

Explanation: You can get a USDA loan to help you finance your home without having to put any funds down..

73.What has helped to lower the number of incidences of fraud involving third-party foreclosure negotiators?

A.Negotiators can collect a fee for showing the foreclosed property

B.Negotiators may collect a fee once a successful negotiation has occurred.

C.Increased negotiator expenses may occur from pre-negotiations.

D.None of the preceding.

Answer: B

74.All and any Outstanding liens and encumbrances can be found on which page of the title insurance binder?

A.A Schedule

B.B Schedule

C.C Schedule

D.D Schedule

Answer: B

75. Is this a personal loan or a business loan if everything in the loan file that is being delivered to a loan originator for financing is incorrect, fabricated, and deceitful?

A.A fixed-rate loan

B.Loan that floats

C.Loan obtained by deception

D.Air Loans

Answer: D

76.Is it a red flag when comparables that are far away from the subject property are used when a rural property is appraised?

A.Yes, the appraisal should include comparables within a 20-mile radius.

B.Yes, comparable properties within a 3-mile radius must be utilized in the appraisal.

C.No, It is not necessary for the appraisal to be a red flag, and it can be approved - as there are no similar properties in the vicinity.

D. None of the preceding

Answer: C

77.What do you call fraud concerns in the mortgage process?

A.Red flags

B.Blue Flags

C.Flags of yellow

D.Flags of white

Answer: A

78.You get a loan request for $484500 on a single-family home, which is more than the traditional mortgage maximum. Which loan will you use to finance this purchase?

A.Jumbo Financing

B.ARM (Alternative Refinancing Mortgage)

C.FHA-insured mortgages

Answer: A

79.A VA loan application is sent to you. Because the property purchase price exceeds $489000, you must determine whether a 0% downpayment is appropriate for this loan application. What decision will you make as a loan originator?

A.0%

B.25%

C.15%

D.5%

Answer: B

80.Which constitutional statute prevents fraudulently claiming through advertising and promotion that the government has sponsored a particular program, item, or service?

A.RESPA (Reform of the Civil Service Act)

B.TILA (Title Insurance and Liability Act)

C.ECOA is a non-profit organization that promotes environmental awareness.

D.GIBA

Answer: B

81.Which legislation is primarily concerned with identifying and combating workplace discrimination?

A.ECOA (Environmental Conservation Agency of the United States) RESPA (Reform of the Civil Service Act)

B. RESPA (Reform of the Civil Service Act)

C.TILA (Title Insurance and Liability Act)

D. HMDA (Health and Medical Devices Act)

D is the answer.

82.A borrower makes a $500,000 purchase. They put down a 25% deposit. The borrower selects an interest rate that is higher than the market rate and receives a 1% closing cost credit. In this circumstance, what is the maximum amount to which settlement costs can be reduced?

A. $2250

B.$3000

C.$2800

D.$3100

Answer: A

Explanation: The loan amount would be $225000 after a 25% down payment. The settlement cost will be reduced by ($225000 x.01) = $2250 with a 1% credit.

83.What is the housing expense ratio of a client with an annual income of $100,000 and housing expenses of $2100?

A.25.2%

B.35.2%

C.30%

D.24%

Answer: D

84.Can a borrower excessively force a lender to refinance solely for his personal benefit without providing the borrower with a real net tangible benefit?

A.Yes, this is permissible.

B.No, a refinance must always provide a net tangible advantage to the borrower.

C.This is authorized for fixed-rate loans.

D.This is permitted in the case of ARM

Answer: B

85.A Commissioner has some reservations regarding a licensee's formal request for justification. What else could he possibly want?

A.Licensee's books and records

B.Licensee's book

C.Licensee's records

D.None of the above

Answer: A

86.What kind of insurance does the guarantor provide to the lender in the event that the lender causes harm to someone?

A.They may submit a claim for compensation for Carelessness, inability, or delinquency.

B.Mistreated, ineptitude, and wrongdoing may result in a claim that can be easily dismissed.

C.Carelessness, ineptitude, and wrongdoing can result in bodily injury to a person.

D.All of the above

Answer: A

87.What happens to the lender if a warranty bond claim is ever paid?

A.They are not permitted to originate until a compensation assurance is acquired.

B.They will be unable to obtain loans for the rest of their lives.

C.They are not allowed to take out a loan for a year.

D.They are qualified to work as a real estate agent

Answer: A

88.How long does it take to remove an MIP?

A.After 9 years

B.After 10 years

C.After 11 years

D.After a period of 12 years

Answer: C

89.What is the most significant benefit of some lenders' capacity to float down?

A.If tariffs fall before the deadline, the borrower can request a one-time tariff reduction.

B.If tariffs fall before the deadline, the borrower can apply for a one-time tariff reduction.

C.Borrower can make plea for a triple of the amount if prices fall after closing.

D.If prices fall after closing, the applicant can request a tripling of the price.

Answer: A

90.After locking in their interest rates, some lenders offer a float-down option to their clients. If the interest rate lowers before the closing date, this allows for a one-time interest rate reduction. What is gathered from customers in exchange for this benefit?

A.This is a complimentary benefit.

B.This is a benefit that comes with an additional point fee at the conclusion of the transaction.

C.Clients are allowed to pay what they choose.

D.Clients must provide a monetary deposit.

Answer: D

91. The loan originator is currently working on a loan for a client who has recently moved employment. Is this behavior a cause for concern?

A.Without a doubt. Change of employment while processing a loan is a red flag.

B.No, this is not a red flag.

C.This is a red flag.

D.This is a case where the white flag should be raised.

Answer: B

CONCLUSION

I appreciate you putting aside the time to read this book and I hope you feel more confident about the mortgage loan originator exam now that you have finished the book. This test is difficult and it distinguishes between people who sincerely desire this goal and those who do not.

A mortgage loan originator's job is both rewarding and challenging. Having a rewarding work with liberty and a high financial income will not be easy. But, I admit, reading this book is just the beginning. Repeat this material until you can recite it in your sleep. I also want you to learn how to recall this information when you need it. My goal is for you to become the best mortgage loan originator you can be, not merely memorize everything.

Previously, you learned about the duties and obligations of a loan originator, as well as the rewards and challenges of the position. But a little challenge is good. You'll need to think creatively and critically frequently. We discussed the test and how to pass it after learning about the job route. The licensing exam should be your primary goal right now since without it, you cannot progress. While the majority, around 60%, pass on the first try, a considerable percentage do not, and must wait 30 days before taking it again. Regrettably, this is time wasted that could be spent on a career.

I want you everyone to ace this test on the first try and significantly raise first-time pass rates. Of course, it takes time and work. You will need to study lengthy hours and be efficient with them. If not, the exercises are pointless. So, start studying using the study techniques in Chapter 2. Examine the requirements for your state's licensure.

The loan origination industry has various rules and regulations. Many of these came about or were revised after the early 2000s misleading practices led many people to lose their houses and even go bankrupt. As a loan originator, you must know these laws to stay within your license's legal boundaries. The regulations also govern loans and advertising. Using proper business ethics is also moral and lawful. There are various ethical ways for a corporation or entity to interact with their competitors.

You must also know the various mortgage products and services available. While standard fixed-rate loans are the most frequent, there are numerous different mortgages that have their own benefits in particular scenarios. Consider your client's present income, savings, and future objectives to make the greatest research-based option for them. A balloon loan or interest-only mortgage can be a better option in some instances, provided the borrower understands the terms and prepares properly.

A mortgage loan originator is self-employed. This implies you must find and keep your own customers. To accomplish so, you must be an expert in your profession and also know how to establish relationships. You must be at ease with your clients. So, act morally. Be there for them. Let them know what you can do for them without being overbearing. You will always be remembered by your clientele.

After reading this book's contents, it's vital to go through the practice questions. While it is nigh-on impossible to know exactly which questions will be on the test, these questions are in the official style so you know what to expect. Examining a large number of practice questions will prepare your thinking for the real thing.

Overall, I wanted to compile all relevant information into one place. But please don't be afraid to use other resources, especially for extra practice questions. My major goal is for you to pass the exam on your first attempt and begin your new profession. The license exam is the biggest hurdle.

Now that you have made it to the end of this book, the next step is to review the information again, recite it, and go back through again. Get your study groups together, find a secluded place with no distractions, and keep reviewing all of this information all the way up to test day. Remember that the more you review, the more this information will make sense. Just going through it once or twice is not acceptable. If you prepare hard for this exam, I have complete faith that you will be successful in your ventures.

If you have enjoyed utilizing this book in your studies, please leave us a 5* review on Amazon or Audible. It helps more than you could ever know!

www.ingramcontent.com/pod-product-compliance
Ingram Content Group UK Ltd.
Pitfield, Milton Keynes, MK11 3LW, UK
UKHW041953190726
13854UKWH00005B/1944